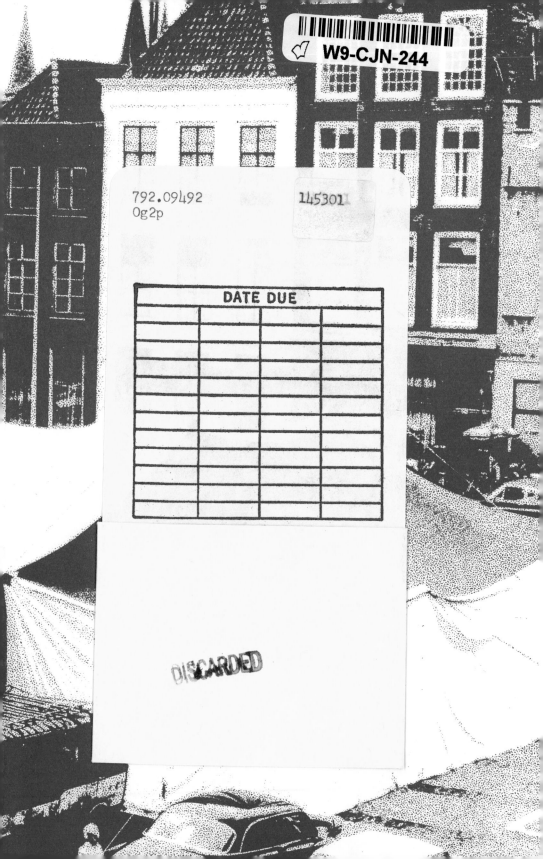

Performance Dynamics and the Amsterdam Werkteater

Performance
Dynamics
and the
Amsterdam
Werkteater

DUNBAR H. OGDEN

With a Foreword
by R.L. Erenstein

University of California Press

Berkeley / Los Angeles / London

University of California Press
Berkeley and Los Angeles, California
University of California Press, Ltd.
London, England

© 1987 by Dunbar H. Ogden

The text of *Avondrood* (*Twilight*) is translated in Chapter 3
and excerpted in Appendix C by permission of
the Coöperatieve Vereniging Het Werkteater,
Spuistraat 2, 1012 TS Amsterdam, The Netherlands;
© 1978.

LIBRARY OF CONGRESS CATALOGING-IN-PUBLICATION DATA

Ogden, Dunbar H.
Performance dynamics and the Amsterdam Werkteater.
Includes index.
1. Werkteater (Amsterdam, Netherlands). 2. Acting.
I. Title.
PN2716.A52W476 1987   792'.09492'3   86-24927
ISBN 0-520-05814-3 (alk. paper)

Printed in the United States of America

1 2 3 4 5 6 7 8 9

To
Alois M. Nagler,
in his tradition of
documents in theater history,
on his eightieth birthday

———

Contents

I

The Werkteater's
Life and Work

Illustrations

Foreword

Good theater is theater that gives expression to the human condition by means that a contemporary audience can recognize. It changes with its era and seeks new forms for its time. It emphasizes the actor as a representative of *homo ludens*, the human being as the player. It investigates fundamental possibilities of expression, and it tries to break through the barriers imposed by time and culture. When it succeeds in making such a breakthrough, it often provokes major changes in performance, such as those that have followed the pioneering work of Stanislavsky, Copeau, Artaud, Brecht, and Grotowski.

As European audiences have known for a decade and a half, all of these challenges have been met brilliantly by the Werkteater of Amsterdam. This innovative company arose in 1969–70, when a dozen already well-trained actors came together in the hope of creating a theater rooted in their own life experiences and devoted to subjects of contemporary social reality. After this remarkably long period of fifteen years together, most of the original Werkteater actors went out individually to work with other people and other groups, transplanting their attitudes and methods to film and television, as well as to other forms of theatrical performance. This book is about their beginnings, their growth, and their maturity as a living organism. Working collectively by means of extensive improvisations—and with no producer, director, or script—they would immerse themselves in a subject chosen by the group and gradually develop a coherent theatrical piece. Among their subjects were the handling of patients in a mental institution, relationships in a home for the elderly, and social taboos about aging and dying. Their shaping of this material was never didactic because they always drew primarily on irreducibly personal experience. In their style of production they rejected illusionistic features such as costumes, sets, and special lighting. They began to address each other on stage by their real names, and sometimes they had men play women's roles and vice versa. They embraced these apparently self-limiting methods as opportunities, as means of forcing the performing itself to carry the message to the audience. They aimed not to "act like" a man in a wheelchair or an old woman in a rest home but to capture that person's state of mind and bring it to life in themselves.

How can we honestly analyze acting of this sort? In the early days of theater research we may have worked almost solely with dramatic texts. Such an approach was acceptable as long as the author was the most important figure in a production and the exclusive aim of the performers was to express the author's ideas as clearly as they could. But when seeking to understand a genuine actors' theater—such as those in ancient Greece and Italy, or the stagings by medieval *joculatores* and the first professional actors of commedia dell'arte—we cannot look at the plays alone, for the source of their strength lies hidden in the evanescent dynamics of performance. Although this fact has been acknowledged for many years, serious students of the theater have only recently begun to find fruitful methods of investigating what really goes on while a piece of theater is being performed.

Professor Ogden is eminently qualified to advance this work. His years of research in Germany, England, Italy, and the Netherlands have given him a solid understanding of the European theater and its creators, and his practical work as teacher and theater person lends sensitivity and subtlety to his appreciation of the actor's craft. Thus in presenting this first full-scale study of the Werkteater, he is able to connect the interests of two types of readers who usually move in different circles—those who study theater and those who create it.

In defining the place of the Werkteater in the modern alternative theater movement, Professor Ogden sheds light on the quest for good theater throughout history. His analysis of the dynamics of Werkteater performances is both comprehensive and concrete: he draws specific examples and illustrations from the entire theatrical oeuvre of this troupe, and he offers us a rare inside view of the development and performance of a single Werkteater play, *Twilight*. By learning in intimate detail how the actors created this play, and only then analyzing the dynamics of its performance, he allows us to gain a surprisingly full awareness of its power.

I believe that many readers will come to marvel at the honesty, intelligence, and emotional stamina of the Werkteater actors, who often speak for themselves in this volume. But actors most of all should welcome this new insight into their craft, and its wealth of intensely practical observations on the mystery of effective performance.

R. L. Erenstein
Institute for Theater Research
University of Amsterdam

Preface

————

$\mathbf{M}$y personal experience with the Amsterdam Werkteater began
when I attended one of their performances in the fall of 1974. An
audience of about 150, mostly young people, crowded into an
upstairs room in a remodeled factory building, a room furnished
only with wooden risers and folding chairs. There was no stage.
We sat in a semicircle around a floor space that contained nothing but four chairs. Then a group of actors walked in and began
to play out a loosely connected series of scenes set in a mental
institution: two doctors throw a patient into total confusion with
their own quarrel over psychiatric treatment; a staff member
holds a party for the withdrawn patients, but when some wild
fun erupts, his superior breaks it up with vindictive criticism
and the patients retreat into silence; after hospitalization for a
nervous breakdown, a girl returns to her home and tries to become part of the family again, but she fails. The actors wore
their work clothes—sweaters, jeans, sneakers—and called each
other by their real names. When the production ended, after an
hour and a half, the performers mingled with the audience for
informal conversation over coffee or beer—answering questions, asking what people thought about the scenes, and talking
candidly about themselves and the difficulties of their work.

The Werkteater as I have described it existed from 1970 to
1985. I have concentrated on that part of its total life cycle, beginning with the 1970 founding, in order to illustrate important
principles of theater in general. For the 1986–87 season three
original members remained in an otherwise rather new company
of thirteen. That group continued to use the approaches devel-

oped by the founders, but environment and personal history together had changed. The change had come rapidly and radically. At the end of the volume, I indicate very briefly a few of the ways in which original members have continued the Werkteater process in different performance environments.

The piece I saw that night in 1974, called *In a Mess*, was one that the actors also presented in mental institutions, for staff members and sometimes patients as well. Occasionally they would give performances in prisons (*Crime*), special schools, hospitals (*Scared to Death* and *You've Got to Live with It*), and homes for the elderly (*Twilight*). The actors would take their audiences, often in one sitting, not only across the forbidding fields of suffering and death but also into the funny, ironic, and joyous realms of comedy. They evolved performances—each rather like a collage, consisting of a sequence of scenes and quick sketches linked together by a particular theme—about women's roles (*It's Only a Girl*), office workers (*Good Morning, Sir*), homosexuals (*One of Them*), street people (*Hello Fellow*), orphanages (*Nobody Home*), and people in prisons (*Crime*), psychiatric institutions (*In a Mess*), and hospitals (*In for Treatment*).

During the summer months the company would leave Amsterdam and travel about the country, performing under a circus tent set up in marketplaces. In the morning the actors would give a freewheeling acrobatic show in which the local children would participate; in the afternoon they would give another show for older children; and in the evening they would put on a broad farcical piece for the whole town. In their farces—such as *A Party for Nico*, with its contretemps between a liberal son and his conservative family, and *A Hot Summer Night*, with its hilarious exposure of tensions within a husband-and-wife comedy team—one sees a kind of modern commedia dell'arte. In all their work, by keeping their focus always on the actor, they captured over the years a range of characters and situations that span what Balzac called *La Comédie humaine*.

In the acting I saw on my first visit to the Werkteater there were no virtuoso displays of language, no Shakespearian cascades of words, only ordinary speech with vibrations of extraordinary meaning. There was no elaborate blocking or formality of movement, only everyday gestures that captured inner moods with the condensed power of haiku. I saw no major and minor roles being played, no stars and bit players, and above all no "character types"—only ordinary-looking persons of stunning presence, whose every move seemed absolutely personal and yet somehow universal. I came away full of admiration and full of questions. How do they do it? Is it possible to find out, so that other actors could learn from them? Is this a glimpse of the theater of tomorrow?

The present volume is the result of a long preoccupation with these questions. Some things in it will appeal to any reader who takes more than a casual interest in the work of pioneering artists in our culture. As I suggest in Chapter 1, the Werkteater company may have achieved together what many pioneers— Stanislavsky, Copeau, Artaud, Brecht, and Grotowski—have sought to bring to the theater through their individual efforts. But what I have written here is primarily for actors and students of the theater. For them, I have tried to make my analyses and descriptions as specific as possible.

Although pictures on a page can barely suggest what an actor does while performing (the Werkteater's films and videotaped performances come much closer), I have illustrated specific points in my text with photographs of these actors at work. Chapter 2 is an insider's description of the Werkteater's working process, a log that charts the company's course for nearly a year as they developed their play *Twilight*. Chapter 3 presents the text of *Twilight*, transcribed and translated into English from a performance that I tape-recorded. On pages facing the text of the play, the actors themselves describe the inner resources they draw upon at certain moments of performance and discuss the dynamics of playing particular scenes.

In Chapters 4 through 6, I propose three conceptual keys to the power of the Werkteater actors. The first key is *playmaking*, for the actors' creative work begins not with a product—the script of a play—but with a process, a democratic and terribly demanding way of working together. The second key is *meta-*

morphosis, a dynamic exchange that takes place simultaneously on three levels: between one actor and another, between an actor and his or her role, and between the performers and the members of their audience. The third key, and the goal of this kind of acting, is the experience of *recognition.* It begins when an actor's deep work leads him or her to discover a wellspring of energy inside a role. It completes itself when a theatergoer gets a jolt of that energy, and with it a sudden insight into what it means to be alive.

In Chapter 7, I isolate the essential characteristics of all the Werkteater's creations. The concluding essay, Chapter 8, suggests features of the Werkteater that may point toward the theater of tomorrow.

Acknowledgments

———

Throughout the processes that have contributed to the making of this book, each individual member of the Werkteater has been very candid and very generous.

Hans Man in't Veld from the Werkteater has gone over the entire book with me and has seen the work to its completion. The other company members in the Werkteater's troika, the steering committee, have reviewed it as well, while individual actors have checked their own comments as quoted.

Rob Erenstein, Annegret Ogden, and Robert Sarlós have read drafts of the essays. Over and over again they have goaded me into asking myself those two questions fundamental to every author: What do you really want to say? And to whom? After I had written the essays, Shireen Strooker from the Werkteater visited in Berkeley for half a year, and through her work with students here she reinforced and strengthened my own thinking about some of the concepts that underlie the book. Toward the end Gene Tanke took a still sprawling manuscript and put his clear mind and his sharp pruning shears to it. It has been with tact, patience, and a wonderful sense of humor that Ernest Callenbach has brought the manuscript to—and then through—the University of California Press. In the later phases Rose Vekony has stood beside him with solid editorial work. Behind them lurk two anonymous readers whose incisive critiques, meticulous far beyond the call of duty, prompted two major rewrites. Finally Paul Ogden leaped in and taught me how to use a word processor, and then the very gifted designer Wolfgang Lederer gave the book its look.

In addition, I would not have been able to complete this book in its present form without special professional assistance from the following people: Ben Albach, Eric Alexander, Cobi Bordewijk, Marian Buijs, Hans Croiset, Marianne Erenstein, Bruce Gray, Jac Heijer, Wiebe Hogendoorn, Benjamin Hunningher, Eric O. Johannesson, Jacques Klöters, Emmy Koobs, Ralf Långbacka, Eleanor Lauer, Sam McDaniel, Ida Mager, John Peereboom, Willy Pos, Anita van Reede, Henri Schoenmakers, James Stinson, Henny de Swaan, Han Vije, Agaath Witteman, Sabrina Klein Yanosky, and Hanneke Zeij. On this campus Johan Snapper and Jan and Monique Visser have been genial hosts to Dutch and Flemish people and culture.

For the photographs I am indebted to Catrien Ariëns (Figures 31, 41, 42), Cas Enklaar (25), Bruce Gray (1–21), J. de Haas (44), KLM Staff Newspaper, *Wolkenridder* (37, 38), Wim Riemens (40), Niek Verschoor (36), Dagmar Voss (33), Werkteater (22, 24, 28, 30, 32, 45), L. P. F. Weyman (29), Charlot Wissing (23, 34, 35, 39, 43), and Ria van der Woude (26, 27).

I

The
Werkteater's
Life
and Work

1

Introduction

The Werkteater ensemble was formed in 1970 by a dozen professional actors and actresses who had left various companies in order "to work in a new way," as they put it. At the outset they tried a number of techniques for developing themselves as performers and worked up a number of projects—self-made one-acts, children's theater, and clown pieces. By February of 1972, when they previewed their first major play created by the entire company (*In a Mess*), they had evolved their fundamental processes and attitudes.

According to the company's approach, the ensemble members developed their plays without help from outside playwrights or directors: they concentrated on the actors and gave relatively little emphasis to scenery and costume. In performance the actors sought intimate and direct contact with their audiences. The company's plays do not have an overt political thrust; they tell personal stories, most of which have a strong social impact. Their home theater in Amsterdam was a renovated factory building. Today's newly constituted Werkteater still uses it. They also performed in various institutions, and each summer they traveled around Holland with their annual tent show. Since about 1978, the Werkteater actors began making feature-length films and shorter pieces for television. Over the years they averaged nine or ten projects a season. (A chronology of their productions is given in Appendix A; their performances in international festivals and the various awards they have received are listed in Appendix B.) In 1982 the company had thirteen members, nine of them founders; and for the 1984–85 season it added Werkteater II, a junior company led by Shireen Strooker. In 1986–87 three founding members remained. I am discussing the Werkteater here from 1970 to 1985.

In order to describe what is truly distinctive about the contribution of the Werkteater actors, it will be helpful to look first at the context in which they have worked—the alternative theater movement of recent years. Since the 1970s, two major trends have become discernible in the new work of alternative theater groups. In the first trend, which we might call visual theater, spectacle dominates. One thinks of Robert Wilson, who creates a kind of *Gesamtkunstwerk;* of the force of huge figures in Peter Schumann's Bread and Puppet Theater; of the epic histories by Ariane Mnouchkine in Paris and Peter Stein in Berlin; of the violent grotesques of the Squat Theater, which has moved from Budapest to New York City; and of the proliferation of all sorts of performance art in the United States and Europe.

The second trend we might call actors' theater. In Europe, Jerzy Grotowski has focused on himself as playmaker and on Ryszard Cieslak, his chief actor, as performer. Cieslak became a kind of alter ego—Grotowski is the mind and Cieslak the body. In the United States, Richard Schechner and his Performance Group have likewise laid stress on the presence and the experience of the performer. In both cases there has been a tendency to create so-called rituals or theatrical rites.

Peter Brook has been a prophet and practitioner within both trends. He has generated visceral power in *Marat/Sade* and the spectacle of play in *A Midsummer Night's Dream;* more recently, in *The Ik* and *Carmen,* he has delved into the life of the person as actor. In *The Ik* he undertook anthropology as theater, prodding his cast to make up their own language and to discover, as the African tribe of the Ik had actually discovered, what happens to human relationships when people are forced into the coffin of starvation.

Brook's stripped-down version of Bizet's opera *Carmen,*

which opened in his Bouffes du Nord theater in Paris in 1981–82, called attention to the individuality of each player. Seven people acted and sang the piece on a given night. But three or four actor-singers were assigned to each role, so that on three successive nights a Don José might play opposite three different Carmens. In rehearsal Brook emphasized the personality differences of the actors, so that the inner dynamics of the moments on stage would vary depending on who was in the cast. Moreover, none of the actors addressed the audience with that all-too-familiar subtext of many opera singers: "I'm a prima donna performing a difficult feat for you." Brook and his actors let the audience perceive human qualities that go much deeper than that.

Brook's production of *Carmen* not only stressed the role player within the role, which is so much a part of new theater today, but also connected the audience with a team spirit. The principals remained on the sand-strewn stage almost without a break throughout the entire hour-and-a-half performance. Eleanor Blau has described some of the processes.

And they are constantly in movement—walking, tumbling, fighting—while singing, a feat that has required group practice not only at the start of the [New York] season but in three-quarter-hour sessions . . . before each performance, on a carpet backstage.

Besides calisthenics, the sessions include exercises to improve mental agility. For example, cast members sit in a circle passing along gestures. One snaps his fingers, say. And as all in turn imitate him, someone else taps a forehead, and that is added on until perhaps half a dozen movements are being executed at once by everybody.

"The aim," explains Emily Golden [one of the Carmens], . . . "is to develop emotional and psychological acuity. It's not really for physical coordination. You develop concentration. Peter Brook's idea is that every person needs to be as attuned to one person as [to] the next."

It is precisely this teamwork that engaged the audience in its energies. Moreover, because only a limited number of movements and gestures were set for each actor-singer, a considerable amount of improvisation took place during performances. Blau cites this example: "Cynthia Clarey says that as Carmen, she never knows whether Don José will get up right away to light her cigar, or, having lit it, turn and walk away. 'If he did turn away,' she said, 'I would have to do something to get his attention. For example, I could blow smoke at him.'"[1]

Brook's production of *Carmen* is also one manifestation of a renaissance in the active and sustained collaboration between performers of plays and writers of plays. With Bizet's traditional material, Brook and his actors have become new playwrights. Other examples suggest the international range of this trend. Out of intense experimentation by a group of actors, Caryl Churchill in Great Britain has composed *Cloud 9* and *Fen*. In the United States, Megan Terry and Jean-Claude van Itallie have drawn impulses for their company-created pieces from the work of Joseph Chaikin's actors. Richard Schechner and his Performance Group have linked up with various playwrights. And on the West Coast, the San Francisco Mime Troupe has used these methods in constructing most of its productions, and a group called A Traveling Jewish Theater develops collagelike performances from Jewish history, religious observances, and folklore. Recent American and European audiences have acclaimed the rollicking power of two black actors from South Africa—Percy Mtwa and Mbongeni Ngema—in *Woza Albert!*, written by them in collaboration with Barney Simon. Perhaps the most striking illustrations of this new movement in playwriting lie in the work of the South African playwright Athol Fugard. In describing how he developed his *Orestes*, he writes: "The three actors and myself disappeared into a rehearsal room and ten weeks later we came out and gave our first 'exposure.'" That event changed his life: "It is one of the most important experiences I have had in theater." For Fugard, the discovery of this mode became "the bridge between small-scale improvisational works" such as *The Coat* and "the more ambitious" *Sizwe Bansi Is Dead* and *Master Harold . . . and the Boys*. Actors, he says, "are as precious as a Stradivarius for me."[2]

1. Eleanor Blau, "How the Multiple Casts of 'Carmen' Came to Harmonize," *New York Sunday Times*, 26 February 1984, H3, H6.
2. Russell Vandenbroucke, "Athol Fugard: The Director Collaborates with His Actors," *Theater* 14, no. 1 (Winter 1982): 38.

The Werkteater and
the Alternative Theater Movement

In the techniques it developed over its fifteen years, the Werk-teater of Amsterdam also restored the theater to the actor and the creation of the play to the actor-playwright. But, compared to the other groups we have mentioned, the Werkteater went further and deeper, over a longer period of time, in exploring the primary role of the actor. Throughout each of its productions a conscious subtext looms large: "We are here together, actors and spectators, at a stage event." Film director Mark Rydell (*The River*) has said, "I believe that people are the ultimate drama and human relationships are the stuff of life. . . . The engagement between two beings gives you the strength to continue in a horrendous world."[3] He could have been talking about the Werkteater company, for they rediscovered elemental human links between the audience member and the actor. While giving the play to the actor, they were giving the theater to the audience.

More than any other long-standing professional group in Europe and America, the Werkteater highlighted the human qualities of the person who is acting: his or her presence, characteristics, skills, relations with others, imaginings, and rememberings. Unlike the troupes mentioned earlier, the Werkteater had no dominant leader, no stage director, and no writer of plays. Instead, by choosing a different actor-member—whom they called a "stimulator"—to guide the development of each project, the actors themselves functioned as corporate playwright. The group thus became responsible for the play as well as for the performance.

When staging a written drama, actors normally start with the script. They begin by studying speeches and scenes and then attempt to find connections between themselves as persons and the characters they will play. They move from outside to inside

3. Mark Rydell quoted by Dan Yakir, "Story of Courage, Strength, Disaster," in "Datebook," *San Francisco Sunday Examiner and Chronicle*, 15 January 1984, 34.

themselves. The Werkteater actors did just the opposite. They began with their own relationships and their own imaginings, and then sought dramatic expression for them in speeches and scenes. They started on the inside, with the self, and moved to the outside, seeking form. That process, in Stanislavsky's terms, was their *deep work.*

Deep work requires the whole troupe to have unshakable trust in the individual actor. By investing the actor with the power to create the text and the emotional thrust of the play, the Werkteater asserted the value of the individual person behind the artist. Giving this much power to the actor, of course, involves a risk: it also assumes that within each actor, the artist is capable of moving beyond the person. But what distinguished the Werkteater actors from their counterparts in most improvisational theater was precisely their long training and careful preparation, which is what enabled them to do the deep work their process requires. In 1970, most of the founders of the Werkteater were already professionally trained and had enjoyed some personal success with important companies in the Netherlands. They were inventive professionals who were willing to give up something in order to discover a new way of working. Their immediate aim was not even to perform in public; it was to develop their power as actors. They say that they disliked the tyranny of the director and the practice of role assignment, and that they wanted to devote themselves to research, rehearsal, and role development. They did not begin by wanting to make plays. Playmaking was a process they fell into.

Organizationally, the Werkteater functioned as a democratic collective. All decisions about policy and procedure were voted upon by all members, while day-to-day administrative matters were handled by a troika and an administrative assistant. Two of the actors rotated every three months in the troika; one remained there permanently. Under normal conditions they rehearsed for about five hours each day, primarily developing improvised scenes and taking training exercises—voice technique, gymnastics, circus acrobatics, and yoga. Exercises with particular coaches were arranged to meet the special demands of the piece they were evolving at the moment. During their first two years they concentrated on working together and gave few public performances. In 1974, the company of fourteen included eleven of the founding members. By then about 70 percent of the Werkteater's expenses were covered by a subsidy from the Dutch government, and 10 percent of their costs were paid by the city of Amsterdam. Box office receipts—and later profits from film and television—provided the remaining 20 percent of the funds in their annual budget.

The Werkteater as an Alternative Theater

The Werkteater assimilated many techniques of the innovators of alternative theater, but the experience, personalities, and attitudes of the company generated the group's distinctive character. For instance, whereas alternative theater in general tends to emphasize visual effects, including the use of the actor more for visual than for psychological presence, the Werkteater stressed verbal language. Its rather sparing use of everyday speech often created a kind of minimalist poetry, and scripts have been published for several of their productions—*Scared to Death, You've Got to Live with It, Twilight,* and *You Are My Mother.*[4] By contrast, published versions of collective creations by other theater groups, such as Grotowski's, are quite rare. Also, the Werkteater's scripts are products of its process, not working tools; a script did not exist until it was transcribed from the tape of a public performance. Of course, other major figures in the alternative theater movement—Dario Fo in Italy, Athol Fugard in South Africa, and Robert Wilson in the United States—have

---

4. Daria Mohr, ed., *Het Werkteater, drie stukken* (Amsterdam: Van Gennep, 1979). This collection contains texts in Dutch of: *Scared to Death, You've Got to Live with It,* and *Twilight (Als de dood, Je moet er mee leven, Avondrood).* The text of *Avondrood (Twilight)* as published in the Dutch collection differs in some details from the text translated in the present volume because the text in the Dutch collection was taken from a later performance and adapted for publication.

Joop Admiraal, *U bent mijn moeder* (Amsterdam: International Theater Bookshop, 1982) (*You Are My Mother*). German translation, *Du bist meine Mutter,* trans. Monika Thé (Amsterdam: International Theater Bookshop, 1983).

stressed verbal language. But they are individual play-writers, whereas the Werkteater functioned as a corporate playmaker.

Another characteristic is that the Werkteater emphasized the presence of the individual on stage and sought some revelation of the inner self and some open contact with members of the audience. It did not use the performer as a symbolic element in choreography, or as an isolated body, face, voice, or mask. This tendency reflected the traditional background of the Werkteater actors, most of whom received their formal training at the Amsterdam Theater School.[5] This school used the psychological approach of Stanislavsky as a foundation for character work and scene study, but it also required rigorous training in such traditional areas as voice and speech and movement. When they first started coming together in 1969–70, the Werkteater actors were influenced by the work of such people as Joseph Chaikin at the Open Theater, who experimented with improvisational structures as instruments of collective creation and emphasized the presence of the actor as distinct from the dramatic character. In addition, one of the Werkteater actresses, Yolande Bertsch, had taken some early training with Grotowski in Poland, and she introduced her colleagues to Grotowski's "personal concert"—an individual presentation-of-self exercise that became a basic working method of the whole troupe: one or more company members would evolve a personal scene that would then be linked to other scenes and eventually shaped for public performance.

Werkteater plays, which usually took the form of a collage of scenes, always contained immediately recognizable human stories. The actors were not interested in outrageous physical acts per se, like those in the Performance Group's *Dionysus in 69*, or in multimedia events like those staged by the Squat Theater. In their summer tent shows they did use acrobatics and often a lot of light and music, but at the center they portrayed people whom their audiences knew.

While the Werkteater's plays focused on an identifiable hu-

---

5. As exceptions to this pattern, one of the company members studied singing at the Music Conservatory of Amsterdam, one trained at the Amsterdam Cabaret School, and one came from a design school in Belgium.

man story, their performances drew on a careful attention to physical technique. Yolande Bertsch had also studied with the French mime Jacques Lecoq, and Peter Faber had begun his career, while still a teenager, as a clown and a solo mime performer. These two brought to the Werkteater a strong feeling for body language and physical discipline. Over the years company members continued to train once or twice a week with a pair of circus acrobats, partly in order to include a few simple acrobatics in their performances, but chiefly in order to maintain and improve physical conditioning, teamwork, balance, and timing. They incorporated some of these exercises in their summer farces and their plays for children.

Since the 1960s at least, the alternative theater movement has felt a strong impulse to create political theater.[6] During the early 1970s, in the heat of Vietnam War protests, the Werkteater was often reproached by other young troupes and their followers for not being political enough. In fact, they did engage in some street theater, including a satire they took to the 1972 Olympic Games in Munich; and throughout their life span they punctuated their major work with short pieces critical of the situation in Chile, the Vietnam War, and the nuclear arms race. But, unlike traditional political activists, they believed that the political is ultimately personal—that in order to promote lasting social change, one must get to the heart of the human condition. This attitude found expression in the Werkteater's first major project for the whole company, *In a Mess* (performed 1972–75), which depicts situations in a psychiatric institution. Influenced by their reading of works in psychology by Jan Foudraine and R. D. Laing, the company began simply by exploring ways in which people communicate with each other and by asking themselves why some people are called "normal" and others "abnormal." After they had developed a series of scenes and performed them

6. The San Francisco Mime Troupe was born from this impulse, as was El Teatro Campesino, both of which use techniques inspired by commedia dell'arte. At Stoke-on-Trent in England, Peter Cheeseman and the writer Peter Terson pioneered the musical documentary based on local sources. On the Continent, Dario Fo's plays and performing style reflect an overt drive by several groups toward inciting social and political change. For most efforts in this direction, Brecht continues to serve as prophet and model.

publicly in their regular Amsterdam theater, the Werkteater was invited by a group of psychiatric workers to give a few performances inside psychiatric institutions, for patients and staff members. Although the company had doubts at first—they were only actors, they said, certainly not social reformers, and they knew nothing about institutional work—they eventually did perform as guests in some of these institutions. On these occasions they served as catalysts for discussion, and even, in a few instances, for actual reform. This accidental experience created a pattern for them, in part because they learned so much from it about honesty and adaptability in playing.

Partially in the context of political motivation, alternative theater groups have commonly avoided traditional theaters and theatrical spaces. When Luca Ronconi staged Ariosto's *Orlando Furioso* in the streets of various Italian cities in 1969, he expressed a widespread desire to infuse a theatrical production with the live atmosphere of a nontheatrical environment and to construct a situation with a rather mobile audience. In Poland, Grotowski had been establishing a special environment for each of his productions. In his *Doctor Faustus*, for example, the audience gathered as guests around a huge table that served as the chief playing area. In addition, environmental theater projects have created a variety of relationships between performer and audience, and happenings have used the normal activities that occur in a certain space—such as a busy street corner—as substantive elements in the performance, or even as its main subject.

The Werkteater, too, determined to draw spectators into the performance in some way. Its regular performance space was the informal environment of a renovated factory in Amsterdam, where 150 to 200 chairs partially surrounded the playing area. This setting encouraged immediate eye contact and a very open connection between individual performers and audience members, a dynamic that exactly matched the intimate human qualities of the scenes being presented. Environmental theater and the phenomenon of happenings made the Werkteater especially sensitive to the ambience of performance—the charged atmosphere that can occur when players and spectators meet in a particular place. Their continuing practices of playing in various institutions and of taking their summer tent comedy on tour kept them attuned in very acute ways to the surroundings in which they performed. In an institution they would speak with their audiences, and in a tent they would laugh and banter with them.

The dynamics of a Werkteater performance also encouraged emotional identification with the performers, partly through cause-and-effect plots that promoted the creation of psychologically based characters. The plays usually consisted of a montage of scenes, or the interweaving of little stories, or a sequence of miniature one-act plays. *Waldeslust*, for example, mixes comic episodes that occur among a group of tourists with touching scenes from among a group of handicapped children and their teachers. Each group makes a comment on the other only through the juxtaposition of the scenes: the two never meet. Within the alternative theater movement such plotting is unusual. It differs, for example, from the kaleidoscopic display of occurrences that characterizes such companies as the Living Theater. Kaleidoscopic scene structure derives largely from the theater of the absurd and has its ancestry in Alfred Jarry and Dada.

Much of the alternative theater movement produces autobiographical work. For example, through his primarily visual effects Richard Foreman projects his own private world; and the Squat Theater, by means of its fragmented multimedia displays, constructs personal phantasmagoria from its eleven adults and five children. The Werkteater members also used autobiographical material but in a somewhat different way: each actor sought to connect his or her inner experience with the inner life of the character and the situation he or she was creating. Thus in *Twilight*, a performance about a group in an old people's home, the actors did not play old people. They expressed their own feelings about what it is like to be aging. Of course, many situations and characters in *Twilight* were drawn from their own experiences with older people and were sketched externally from a grandmother or an uncle. But the inner life of the characters belonged to the actors themselves. This inner life is by far the most significant feature of the characters in *Twilight*. Because the

Werkteater actors had evolved techniques for going deep in their exploration of aging, what they revealed about themselves is universally true and caused a sympathetic vibration in all their listeners, regardless of age.

The Werkteater as an Art Theater

The distinguished Finnish director Ralf Långbacka, in an essay entitled "On the Prerequisites for an Art Theater," provides an important perspective on characteristics of the Werkteater and its place in twentieth-century theater. From the past ninety years of theater history, Långbacka singles out six theaters and their leaders: Konstantin Stanislavsky and Vladimir Nemirovitch-Danchenko and the Moscow Art Theater; Bertolt Brecht and the Berliner Ensemble; Giorgio Strehler and Paolo Grassi and the Piccolo Teatro di Milano; Otomar Krejča and the Divaldo za Branou (Theater on the Balustrade) in Prague; Juri Ljubimov and the Taganka Theater in Moscow; and Peter Stein and the Schaubühne am Halleschen Ufer in West Berlin. From an analysis of these six, Långbacka derives eight principles of what he calls an art theater. In addition, he examines the work of several other groups, notably Joan Littlewood and the Theater Workshop; Roger Planchon and the Théâtre de Villeurbanne; Jean Vilar and the Théâtre National Populaire; Peter Brook and his Paris ensemble; and Ariane Mnouchkine and the Théâtre du Soleil in Paris.

Långbacka's focus on the six groups proceeds from his definition of an art theater:

Art in this context does not simply denote a matter of quality; rather by art I refer to the type of theater, like the Moscow Art Theater, which effected renewal of the theater and which functioned in its time and place in a way which gave the theater a meaning as something beyond a place for skilled entertainment.[7]

7. Ralf Långbacka, "Om förutsättningarna för en konstnärlig teater," in *Bland annat om Brecht, texter om teater* (Stockholm: P. A. Norstedt och Söners Förlag, 1982), 279–310.

He contrasts the art theater with what he calls the institutional theater: one that suffers from a lack of ideas and a certain spiritual poverty, and that also often consumes disproportionate amounts of money. Small theaters by no means escape this latter definition. Indeed many try to become more institutional than their large institutionalized competitors. In Långbacka's view, institutional theater stands at one end of a scale and art theater at the other, and between the two extremes there exist many opportunities for effectiveness.

The eight common principles that Långbacka finds manifested in the six art theaters are as follows:

1. An art theater requires a group of people with mutual goals; the group organizes itself around a person or persons who can express the values of the group.

2. An art theater rises in opposition to an old, petrified theater and breaks with the old theater's ideology, playing styles, and production methods.

3. An art theater attempts to reach a new audience, or to change the structure of its audience, as well as to provide a new theatrical experience.

4. An art theater has a clear and selective repertory, built on aesthetic consistency and integrity, in which the individual productions support each other. (No more smorgasbord theater seasons!)

5. An art theater searches for new artistic working methods, methods that will include all the kinds of work done in the theater and all the persons who work in the theater. Often these methods are developed from an ideology and exist in a process of constant renewal and change.

6. An art theater has an external and internal form of organization that strives for the maximum artistic results. The purpose of the organization is to facilitate and support the artistic process rather than simply to maintain an institution.

7. An art theater demands great individual effort as well as collective effort. In conflicts between artistic demands and social demands (such as demands by labor unions), the artistic result must be considered of overriding importance.

8. An art theater focuses on concerns greater than merely maintaining its own existence. An art theater remains an art theater only so long as it succeeds in renewing itself and in maintaining or improving its relationship to the political or social reality from which it arose.

Clearly the Werkteater departs from some of Långbacka's principles. The company members functioned as a true collective rather than as a group gathered around a central authority. As a result, the dynamics of their own personal interactions, and what emerged from them on stage, often differed from the inner dynamics of actors who follow a single strong leader. Three reasons account for this quality: first, their policy was made collectively, and their artistic leadership shifted with their different projects. Second, group members were not only actors but playwrights. Third, everything they did, including the evolution of a body of acting techniques and a core of attitudes about performance, started with the performer.

Like the members of Långbacka's art theaters, the actors of the Werkteater came together in mutual opposition to what they considered stale or ineffectual theater. Specifically, they wanted to discover a new way of working. Among the dozen actors who stayed on after the formative months, the emphasis on the actor and the decision to function democratically arose quite quickly and were never reversed, despite the heavy demands these tactics made on their time and their energies. Unlike the people in Långbacka's six theaters, the Werkteater actors did not originally aim at public productions. Over their first two years they sought and found some simple forms of performance, and eventually they found new audiences for these forms. Despite occasional pressures from different members of the group to stage works by other playwrights, for their first ten years they built their repertory almost entirely from self-made plays. In this process a key to their progress was variety—in duration of projects, types of projects, combinations of members, and periods of project or play development. Variety provided creative stimulus for the group and offered particular means of expression to the individual actors, who differed considerably in personality and interests. A glance at the list of their projects—comedy, tragedy, farce, tent shows, children's plays—might suggest an intention to provide smorgasbord theater, a bit of something for every taste. But they never entertained such a motive. The aesthetic consistency and integrity in their plays, and the careful fitting together of the pieces in the repertory, reflected only the artistic desires of the actor-playwrights.

The Werkteater followed Långbacka's eighth principle, the pursuit of renewal and change, by inviting specific groups to its theater as audiences and by searching out audiences in a variety of places: in public squares, prisons, schools, and community centers. The members of the company recognized very early that much of their power as actors was generated from their social concerns and from the societal contexts in which they played. In the later years they produced some scripted plays and did television and film work, and individual members put on one-person shows and worked in non-Werkteater projects. But in pursuing these new endeavors, they retained their original commitment to risk taking, artistic process rather than institutional maintenance, and a give-and-take with the social and political world in which they lived.[8]

Improvisation and Playmaking
at the Werkteater

The terms *improvisation* and *group improvisation* are often used to mean a style of performance in which actors invent dialogue and scenes in front of an audience. Cabaret members, for instance, ask the audience for a name, a place, or a slogan, and then—possibly after a quick conference—they produce a sketch incorporating the requested elements. American audiences at a popular level came to know this style through sketches developed by Mike Nichols and Elaine May while they worked under Paul Sills at the Second City in Chicago, beginning in the fall of 1959. In the same period Paul Sills's mother, Viola Spolin, was spreading the gospel of theater games to American college and

---

8. Långbacka's principles also serve to suggest the dangers that confront any art theater. We know that petrifaction eventually set in at the Moscow Art Theater, and that a successful art theater naturally tends with time to become more like an institutional theater. The Werkteater's responses to this challenge and the dangers for actors and troupes in taking the Werkteater's particular methods as a model for their own development are briefly described in Chapter 8.

university campuses through her book *Improvisation for the Theater*. Acting instructors and directors were soon using improvisational techniques for several purposes: to free actors from inhibitions, to help them feel an emotional relationship more personally, or to let them discover new gestural or vocal patterns, either in the classroom or during rehearsals of a play.[9]

Although Europeans have known cabaret, which used some of these techniques, since the 1881 opening of Le Chat Noir in Paris's Montmartre, it was Stanislavsky at the Moscow Art Theater who pioneered the use of improvisation in producing a drama—specifically, in producing Chekhov. Stanislavsky was helping his actors find personal psychological roots for the characters and situations that they were asked to play. In 1959, when Jerzy Grotowski, a copy of Artaud in hand, set about establishing his Theater Laboratory in Opole, Poland, he defined theater as "what takes place between spectator and actor."[10] When he used texts of plays, he totally reconstructed them. He erected his performances on foundations laid by mental and physical exercises. Richard Schechner and Joseph Chaikin have used improvisational techniques in developing all of their nontextual productions and have also introduced passages marked for improvisation during the course of public performance.

Despite the company's use of improvisation while evolving one of their pieces, a Werkteater performance showed little variation from night to night. The major improvisational work had taken place earlier. Its method was analogous to that of the Modern Jazz Quartet. In that group the musicians gather to play around with a theme, either a familiar tune or one newly composed. Then after several sessions devoted primarily to improvising, they decide that the piece has achieved a stable structure or framework and is therefore ready for public presentation. When they actually perform it, they leave certain clearly defined sections open for invention by a given player or group of players. During these sections they may play something they in-

9. Viola Spolin, *Improvisation for the Theater* (Evanston, Ill.: Northwestern University Press, 1963).
10. Jerzy Grotowski, *Towards a Poor Theatre* (Copenhagen: Odin Teatres Forlag, 1968), 32.

vented long ago or something they feel inspired to create on the spot. What they do will depend on their mood and their rapport with the audience. Some of their on-the-spot creations will become standard parts of other presentations.

The Werkteater made plays in the same way. The actors developed characters and situations while playing around with their own experiences, dreams, and fantasies. It usually took them about a year to create a major new play. When the troupe formed in 1970, the dozen actors had to find out how to get along with each other in the democratic style that they were choosing. Unlike the Moscow Art Theater, the Theater Laboratory in Poland, the Open Theater, and the Performance Group, they had no dominant leader. Indeed each of them had already rejected the traditional authority of producers and directors. Before the group could even begin to play in front of an audience, each actor had to relearn how to deal with his or her own ego and then with the ego of others. The company members discovered that this very process—with all its struggles, tensions, and fights—kept them playing together.

The Werkteater actors took up improvising as a means of problem solving, a way of dealing with themselves and with each other. But their motives were different from those that prevailed in the self-help therapy groups so popular in the 1970s. They were artists, mature people in full control of the traditional crafts of acting, and they shared a common professional goal. Moreover, they did not practice a sort of popular psychodrama that aims only at releasing individual feelings. Instead, the spiritual roots of their improvisational practice go back to Jacob Levy Moreno, whose "I-Thou concept" became a major element in the thinking of the philosopher Martin Buber.[11] Robert Sarlós has written about Moreno's principles: "Moreno's gospel—for he considered it nothing less—rests on three assumptions: first, that spontaneity/creativity is 'a propelling force of human progress,' second, that 'faith in our fellowmen's intentions' is neces-

11. Moreno, who had revived his Vienna Stegreiftheater of 1921 as the Impromptu Theater in New York in 1931, had an impact on the American Group Theater and on the creativity theories of Neva Boyd and Viola Spolin, which were used in the Federal Theater (1935–39).

sary, and third, that on these two axioms 'a superdynamic community' can be based."[12] To understand the dynamics of the Werkteater, one must look not to contemporary group therapy but to Moreno and to Stanislavsky.

In the company's formative years the Werkteater actors discovered that corporate playmaking can impose a heavy burden on the individual actor: responsibility not only for his or her own performance but also for the creation of the whole play. To ease this burden without seeking refuge in scripts or directors, they decided to assign the primary responsibility for structuring a play to a "stimulator," a fellow actor chosen by all to guide each project. While serving as a stimulator, this person continued to perform as an actor in other works, both those in rehearsal and those in the repertory. The stimulator's role was to help transform individual performances into a play by forcing, goading, coaching, and analyzing, so that the actors could transcend the personal and reach toward the universal with dramatic power.[13] In the sense that one person helped them use their feelings to create a *role*, the Werkteater company resembled a more traditional group. But they went further: they used their feelings to create the living *character* who appeared on stage.

Moreover, personal experience was not the ensemble's only source of dramatic raw material. They balanced it against books and articles by experts in the fields where they ventured. For example, when developing *Twilight*, which deals with aging and dying in contemporary society, they studied relevant works by Elisabeth Kübler-Ross, Margaret Mead, and Jacoba van Velde. For their production of *Crime*, they read the works of a professor of law in The Hague and eventually consulted with him about their play's development. Both before and during the period of public performance, the Werkteater played *Crime* in prisons and in a police academy, where they could discuss it with

12. Robert Sarlós, *Jig Cook and the Provincetown Players* (Amherst, Mass.: University of Massachusetts Press, 1982), 56.
13. As we shall see in the log of the development of *Twilight*, the stimulator does more than take a hand in shaping improvisations during rehearsal months. He or she also leads in the process of selecting and condensing the dozen or more hours of generated material into a public performance of approximately an hour and a half.

an "expert" audience. In a sense the books, experts, and experiences in institutions were to the company what Bizet's opera was to Peter Brook and his multiple casts. For each of their plays, the actors drew on both internal and external resources.

In their book *Improvisation,* John Hodgson and Ernest Richards observe that the qualities needed for the best acting "are also those qualities required for the fullest living."[14] Michael MacOwan, the Principal of the London Academy of Music and Dramatic Art, identifies those qualities as awareness, sensitivity, freedom, and "the self-confidence that comes from the knowledge that every one of us is a unique individual, with a valuable role to play, if we can become ourselves enough to find it, and accept it."

The Werkteater actors sought and exhibited these qualities. And more successfully than any other professional troupe in Europe or America, they developed a way of working that enabled an actor to function effectively as a playwright. In the rest of this book we shall try to reveal the keys to their success.

14. John Hodgson and Ernest Richards, *Improvisation* (London: Methuen, 1966), 11 and ix.

2

The Development of *Twilight*

A Log of the Collective Working Process (1973–1975)

The following account of the development of *Twilight* is offered for several reasons. It is a rare inside view of the creative process and suggests how a piece by the Werkteater developed. The log reveals in some detail the practices that had become standard for the Werkteater and that, when taken together, distinguish it from other companies. And finally, the history provides insight into the genealogy of later Werkteater productions: *You've Got to Live with It* (1977–79), *Scared to Death* (1977–79), *In for Treatment* (1979–80), and *You Are My Mother* (1981–86).

The log is primarily the work of Marian Buijs, an apprentice with the company in 1973 and 1974, who spent a year and a half recording her own observations and talking with the actors who were creating *Twilight*. In collaboration with her, I first translated her notes from the Dutch and added a little material from my own interviews with the actors, including corrections and comments from Shireen Strooker, the company member who served as the troupe's "stimulator" for *Twilight*. In 1985, Marian and I prepared the version contained here to serve the purposes of this book.

20

In September 1973, when the summer tent-theater program had ended, the company discussed the plan for the coming season and decided to work through mid-December according to the following schedule. Three small groups would work together for the first six weeks; then the members would reorganize into three new groups for the remaining six weeks. If these sessions proved productive, six results would be ready by Christmas. Then, from mid-January through mid-May of 1974, the whole company would undertake a joint project.

Everyone wanted Shireen Strooker to serve as the stimulator of the joint project. The function of the stimulator, as spelled out in the Werkteater's *Annual Report, 1971–72* (p. 89), was as follows:

The stimulator encourages creative process in the others by setting up training sessions and exercises, and by giving instructions and suggestions. This person is primarily concerned with helping the actors in their own creative processes, individually and in a group. He or she maintains an overview of the material and attempts to find a line through it. He or she attends to the regular progress of the work by making schedules. The stimulator can ask for assistance in every area, and can even hand over the stimulator's functions to someone else. The difference between a director and the stimulator is this: a director normally begins with a clear concept, a specific view of the piece, whereas the stimulator assists in the development of a mutual vision.

The Werkteater actors formed small groups for various reasons: desire to work on a particular theme, or to work with a particular actor (or actors), or to work with a particular person as stimulator. From mid-September to the end of October 1973, each of the following three small groups started a project:

1. Hans Man in't Veld, Herman Vinck, and Peter Faber (stimulator) evolved a performance for children. They began with an idea about a child's fears, and through improvisations they developed *Glasses and Braces (Brillen en beugels)*, first performed in the Amsterdam theater on 19 December 1973. They continued to play this piece in schools.

2. Rense Royaards, Gerard Thoolen, Helmert Woudenberg,

and Frank Groothof (a guest actor at that time but a member of the company after 1974) devoted themselves to a fairy tale by Kolakowski. With the story as their starting point, they worked out improvisations and individual interpretations. The result was *Gang (Bende)*, which they first presented along with *Glasses and Braces* on 19 December 1973.

3. Joop Admiraal, Yolande Bertsch, Marja Kok, and Daria Mohr worked together with Shireen Strooker as stimulator. They did not address themselves to a given theme but attempted through improvisations to derive something wholly out of themselves. As it turned out, what they developed became the foundation for the later joint project of the whole company.

The sessions for training, improvisation, and rehearsal usually took place five days a week, from ten until two o'clock, with a pause for lunch. Every Friday evening the actors performed in their Amsterdam theater, and during the week they also played in various institutions (schools, homes, prisons) and for special institutional groups. Thus the number of performances per week could vary from two to six, depending partly on the time and energy required to travel to performances.

At least one afternoon or evening each week was given over to a general meeting of all the actors (twelve of them when *Twilight* was being developed). For these decision-making meetings the company developed the following policy: each actor had an equal voice in making all decisions of the company. Except for a secretary, they employed no business or management personnel. To lighten the organizational load, the company operated with a three-person steering committee: two actors served on it for a three-month period and then rotated, with Hans Man in't Veld as the third and permanent member.

The First *Twilight* Group

In the third of the small groups Shireen gave personal "directives" so as to set the actors' creative processes in motion. Later the actors gave each other similar hints and suggestions for exercises. All of these directives and suggestions became quite personal, for the giver as well as the receiver. An actor often tried to find something wholly foreign to the receiver, something he or she had never seen the other actor do. They were determined to break down clichés, to discover and give expression to new resources within each other.

These individual suggestions were similar to the "concerts" led by Yolande during the Werkteater's beginning period—exercises she had learned during a six-month session with Grotowski. Marja commented: "I felt like I was back in the first year of the Werkteater again." The Werkteater's *Annual Report* for 1971–72 explains these exercises:

During the first year we held a series of "concerts" every two months. The term comes from Grotowski. The idea is this: each individual alone prepares something that he wants to show to the others, something that reveals a particular, subjective attitude. For example, you can show something that deeply concerns you: bring along your photograph album, tell about your youth, or do something you always wanted to do—a song, a dance, a monologue, etc. The intention is to give to each other real information about yourself.

The following are some examples of the directives that were passed among the actors. From Shireen to Joop, Yolande, Marja, and Daria: "You meet each other when you die." And: "You come to another planet, where the inhabitants have never seen a human being. You have to show them what a human being is."

From Yolande to Joop: "You're a magician making a comeback, but your trick fails." This instruction connects directly with something that Joop himself wanted to play—"a dirty old man." Joop said, "I did a figure like that once on TV, in a piece by Johnny Speight. I wanted to do that again."

From Yolande to Marja: "You're a crazy old woman. You take ten steps and then you tell a story. You take twenty steps and then you tell a story about your youth." The woman Marja now plays in *Twilight* developed from this directive. Joop said: "She was a strange little woman. Her character comes to the surface when she says she loves to pinch pussy willows with her fingers."

From Joop to Daria: "Play a prima donna who sings an aria,

exuberantly and hysterically." This instruction formed the basis for what Daria still does during the party scene near the end of *Twilight*.

Of course, many such exercises were far from successful, and discoveries did not always occur one immediately after the other. But in general the actors felt that they were working intensely and productively. Shireen became increasingly receptive to their ideas, and everyone was drawn vigorously into the exercises. After a few weeks these actors realized that the idea of "becoming old" and "confronting one's own aging" was inspiring all the members of this small group. Shireen then selected a series of scenes on this theme so that the actors could limit their experimentation.

A year and a half later, Shireen said: "If I thought there was a 'true essence' in an actor's response to a directive, an essence of the character or of the whole thing, I tried to put that into words in a new directive. Once we *named* that essence, we could go on. For example, I might say, 'It's not you who is playing; someone who is dead is playing through you.'" She added: "Nowadays the spiritual aspects of life are very limited and constricted. So much significance is given to material things that when you get old, it seems that there's nothing left, whereas in reality you could have a lot more because the spiritual aspects of life take on greater significance. I want to show something like that."

After the first six-week work period a serious problem arose. Herman, Helmert, and Peter went to play in a film, disrupting their respective groups and leaving Rense and Frank stranded. Rense and Frank decided, therefore, to join the *Twilight* project, but it was an unhappy solution at this point. As newcomers they did not know whether they should do something new or adapt themselves to the already existing patterns. Their collaboration with Shireen's group finally resulted in the creation of a scene of a Christmas celebration in an old people's home, and this scene was then tacked on to the other material. Its connection with the other scenes remained minimal, however, and right before the first scheduled in-house performance the group seriously debated whether to play it at all. They finally decided to retain it.

The First Performance of *Twilight*

The following series of scenes, the prototype or experimental version of *Twilight*, was played on 18 December 1973 to an audience composed mostly of friends and acquaintances of company members. These scenes had been shown once, shortly before, to the other actors.

1. A row of people, sitting on chairs with an alarm clock nearby, wait for something.

2. Someone comes and fetches each of these people, one after the other.

3. Marja tells a story about her youth as she pushes along a doll carriage.

4. Residents of an old people's home congregate.

5. Joop and Marja go off alone together, apparently to have a sexual relation, but instead they defecate with each other.

6. As the directress of the old people's home, Daria throws dirt on the table and then blames each of the residents for the mess.

7. Joop gives a long monologue in which he recommends that a catering service provide excrement.

8. Daria does a suicide scene from an imagined romantic opera.

9. As a nightclub singer, Yolande sings a song about the joys of love. She is dressed in short pants and gold stockings. When she finishes, she gives an interview.

10. Joop attempts a comeback as a magician, but he never gets around to doing a trick.

11. Marja entertains everyone with jokes, despite a high fever.

12. Marja and Yolande help each other put on makeup in preparation for the visiting hour.

13. Everyone participates in a meal.

14. With a fetish Yolande satisfies her longing for love.

15. Daria and Joop hold a séance.

16. The group performs a revue song about life's end.

17. On Christmas Eve the old people celebrate together by putting on a Christmas play.

The reaction of the audience as well as the group members themselves was generally enthusiastic. Rense said, "We did manage to get past a number of stereotypes. Theater conventions were well used, and in a new way." Helmert liked the performance because of its "freedom and power of expression," and felt that "the individual experiences of the players came through in a subliminal way." But Herman, who did not share the generally positive reaction, objected strongly: "Terrible. I find this a regression to theatricality that I can't stomach in any way. Superficial and superfluous."

In fact, except for the actor's approach to his or her role, there was a certain return to theatricality. For the first time in its history the Werkteater had used costumes and lighting effects. Some, like Herman, felt that this placed a barrier between actors and audience, making direct communication impossible and thereby rendering the performance superficial. But others saw it differently. In February 1974, Daria said she thought this theatricality "really derived from within the content of the scenes. You can't hold a séance at all in full light. Moreover, we enjoyed the feeling that we were doing something forbidden. That added tension."

For the most part the actors thought that in *Twilight* they could communicate with an audience not by "playing a character" but rather by vanishing into the character they had created—that their energy for interaction with the audience should come not straight from the actor as an individual (as tended to be the case in *In a Mess*, 1972), but rather from the character. Yet they disagreed among themselves about how best to create a figure on stage, and they had various opinions about whether the Werkteater should do any more performances in the relatively

theatrical style of *Twilight*. In the end the first *Twilight* of
18 December 1973 was a loose string of scenes, held together
thematically or associatively, and the actors were surprised by
the generally favorable reaction to it.

Twilight and the Whole Company

On 14 January 1974, the whole company decided to take up the
Twilight project with Shireen as stimulator. They agreed on the
following principles: (1) The subject or theme must emerge or-
ganically out of the troupe. (2) The basic means of creative development used in the small groups should be applied to the entire ensemble. (3) Space for individual choice and development
must be preserved at all costs. Shireen and various members of
the group held informal conversations and gradually expressed
personal wishes and affinities. In this way Shireen collected material she could use in giving directives.

The actors wondered whether they could begin without a
firm theme or subject and still succeed in creating a coherent
piece. But they were determined not to abandon their most fundamental commitment as actors—to express only what they found
within themselves as individuals. They had already learned from
their experience with *In a Mess* that a group project does not
necessarily require the whole group to work together all the
time, and they knew they could arrange a communal work schedule. Some of their expectations, however, were in conflict. The
people from the first *Twilight* did not want to give up what they
had developed in their small group, and Shireen, now the stimulator of the ensemble, wanted to carry on with the techniques
they had used there. But others wanted to start out fresh and not
worry about having to adapt to processes and ideas that had
already been developed. Somehow they managed to set this
problem aside and conduct themselves as if everyone were beginning from the same point; indeed they never discussed the
issue again.

During their first two weeks of work together, 15–26 January 1974, individual actors pursued various ideas. Joop wanted to do something that dealt with the care of a dying person.[1] He worked with Yolande and two apprentices on such a scene, which slowly evolved through improvisations into two parts: a doctor tells the family that the patient is incurable; and the family then goes to visit the patient. Despite intense labor, the scene began to disintegrate. One of the apprentices even wrote down the text, and they worked from the written draft. The scene was performed at the first Evening Workshop but then dropped, because it deviated too much in a thematic sense from the other scenes being developed. Joop proposed that half the company use the terminally ill figure as the basis for a project that could eventually be played in hospitals, but his proposal was rejected since it conflicted with the earlier agreement to create a project involving the entire company. A month later Yolande said: "There was something crazy about that scene: it always went much better among ourselves than with an audience."

Rense wanted to work with Peter on a scene about love. Improvisations led them to the subject of a frustrated relationship. For years two men share the same office, harboring an unspoken affection for each other. As little incidents are slowly magnified in the scene, their real relationship becomes clear. Eventually the actors presented this scene in several Evening Workshops. But because the public did not perceive the connection with the other scenes, this particular interaction was progressively shortened. In the present *Twilight* all that remains of it are a few snatches of Peter and Rense singing together and sharing a kiss.

Herman wanted to evolve a scene with Marja. Shireen gave them a directive—"You are two angels on a grave"—and the actors developed a scene from improvisations. Two angels look down to earth and begin to manipulate events. They watch with childlike curiosity as human beings die, and they playfully cause small occurrences that have major consequences. For example, a

---

1. This was the seed of what five years later became the Werkteater's feature-length film *In for Treatment*. In December 1974, eleven months after the whole company had begun work on *Twilight*, Joop was granted a leave of absence in order to care for his own father, who was dying of cancer.

woman attempts to suffocate herself with gas, but a dog picks up the odor and comes running, threatening to alert others. The woman is about to fail in her suicide attempt, but the two angels put the dog on another scent so that the woman can do what she wishes. The scene was played once at an Evening Workshop and then dropped.

Shireen also gave improvisations to the ensemble as a unit, and the actors adopted a device that had proved successful at an earlier stage: the players would draw lots to decide who would think up a name, a quality, a way of dressing, and an activity for a colleague. At the outset the company was divided in half, but both halves concentrated on events that might occur in the sitting room of an old people's home. Half of the company worked on a situation in which the old people wait for breakfast. They are sleepy, and during the night a storm has shattered a windowpane. This improvisation was always called "the storm." In the scene worked on by the other half, a pathetic widower dies in the sitting room without anyone's noticing it; after their shock of discovery, the others, with some embarrassment, begin to appropriate his personal belongings. Later this scene came to be known as "the Osdorf scene," after the name given to Helmert, who played the widower.

Within these group improvisations the actors discovered seeds for characters beginning to grow. As they tested a variety of character elements for their colleagues' reactions, they found emerging individual qualities and depths of "becoming old"— different inner sensations and different ways of moving. The differences among the players themselves served as a stimulus, and those who were farther along in their individual exploration could assist and inspire the others. In contrast, sometimes an actor who was more at ease in a given improvisation could inhibit the others through the very force of his or her practice.

After two weeks Shireen suggested another approach. To encourage a high level of spontaneity, she asked small groups to develop something very rapidly in one morning session and show it to the others the next day. Two of the resulting scenes ran as follows. Helmert and Marja, having made contact through a newspaper advertisement, meet in order to see whether they really want to go on a vacation together, and if so, under what conditions. Daria and Jaap (a guest actor) do a Frankenstein-like number in which a vaudeville artist with a strong German accent performs an act with a talking doll. The doll slowly comes to life and seems to be a concentration camp victim under the spell of the camp doctor, who had appeared to be the vaudeville performer.

No one expected these exercises to make direct contributions to the central project. They were intended to invigorate the actors and to shake loose new ideas. On seeing the first results, Shireen suggested that, rather than discussing them, they undertake another three rounds of instant scene-making, absolutely without critique. The subsequent exercises produced an enormous store of raw material. Shireen said: "If we leave spontaneous ideas undiscussed, they have a way of feeding us unconsciously. Discussion at this early stage can tend to make you too aware. We only want to feel ourselves free, so that we can discover new resources. We don't want to fear that nothing will come of it. We want the mutual daring to leap into the uncertain, with no thought about the result."

Clearly, Shireen wanted to follow the basic practices that had been successful in the small groups, but this unrestricted exploration, conducted with "no thought about the result," was hard to sustain in a large group. The day after the instant scene-making concluded, the group complained about "running wild" with disjointed scenes and said they feared they were losing a sense of the project's totality. Working up acts that would not fit the whole, such as the office scene between Rense and Peter, seemed a waste of effort, a dissipation of energy. The enlarged size of the group had increased the problems. Many of the actors urged that henceforth all new ideas for scenes should contain thematic material that could undoubtedly be tailored to fit into the whole production.

In response Shireen aimed her directives right at the character that each actor was evolving within the group improvisations, such as the "storm" and "Osdorf" scenes. She said she wanted to help the actors to generate impulses from moments in the lives of these old people. Two of the improvisations that resulted from these new directives were as follows: (1) Herman begins to write a letter to his father, Helmert, requesting financial assistance. But he does not get far because the two of them meet, quarrel, and overwhelm each other with reproaches. (2) Daria and Marja are two old women who read romantic novels to each other. They identify with the fictitious characters and finally attempt to outdo each other in reciting their own imagined adventures with men.

By the beginning of February, Shireen believed that through this focus on developing individual characters for the old people, they could accommodate nearly everything they invented. Improvisation in the large group, its two halves now joined, centered on the visiting hour in the home, where the feelings and rhythms of the old people could be contrasted with the energies of youth—as in a sketch in which two of the old people meet a young couple and offer themselves as babysitters. In this way some of the realities of "being old" appeared in a broader social context.

Shireen now issued a flood of instructions for quick sketches. For example, one morning she gave the actors half an hour to work up an improvisation using music. The results were diverse and unexpected. To give only one sample: Gerard enters, dripping wet and wrapped in a towel; he sings a song in which he says that he has just tried to drown himself in a canal, and that despite his misery he is happy someone fished him out. This piece, like many others, was later discarded. Shireen was impulsive, spontaneous, and optimistic. She seemed to be everywhere, giving hints and fresh suggestions, holding informal personal conversations, searching for ways to accommodate individual wishes, and watching for petrified moments.

As the actors worked in this way through February, they also began to look for information and background material in books, such as *On Death and Dying* by Elisabeth Kübler-Ross, *Male and Female* by Margaret Mead, and *The Big Ward* by Jacoba van Velde. They sought not factual detail but deeper insight into the environment of an old people's home. The most effective technique for digesting this reading proved to be the "street interview." A character would be questioned by another company member about his or her life, past and present; occasionally a bystander would interrupt to express an opinion of his own about old people—usually an opinion that reflected generalized social attitudes or prejudices about the elderly. The actor therefore had to practice keeping a double focus—on himself or herself and on events in the surroundings. The spontaneous interruptions from bystanders could elicit strong subjective views from the actor, while the main interview could encourage him or her to explore new depths in the character being played.

By the end of February, so much raw material had been gathered that the ensemble felt an urgent need to show it to the public in Evening Workshops. These workshop presentations, which had been an integral part of the actors' lives for the past two seasons, offered two great benefits. First, the experience of performing in public could help the performers find stronger lines of continuity in their material. Despite the informal atmosphere, the actors said that they felt considerably more tension at a workshop performance than they did at rehearsals, for here they had to make their separate performances contribute to the whole production. The presence of spectators demanded greater clarity from them, so that a stronger cohesion among the scenes often resulted. In fact, rather muddy pieces would frequently take on new coloring and suddenly fit cleanly into the mosaic. Second, by assessing the alternating flow of current between spectators and actors, the company hoped to discover ways to make major substantive improvements in the performance. In this manner the company's audiences played a role in their playmaking process.

The Evening Workshops

On 27 February 1974, the Werkteater sent out the following notice, especially to institutions and individuals concerned with older people:

Almost daily now we are working on a new project with Shireen Strooker as stimulator. It does not have a title yet, but it deals with people in the last phase of their lives, people who have no more influence on events that occur in the world but who are still filled with desires and want to deal with the unfinished business in their lives.

The entire company is working on this project, along with two guests: Jaap Hoogstra and Jytte Justesen [an apprentice].

In March and April we want to organize with audiences a number of Evening and Morning Workshops. We will present developed material, and we hope that a great deal of reaction and information will come from the audience groups. The dates are March 5, 19, 20, and 27, and possibly Friday mornings, if there are requests from special groups (school people, working young people, older people, etc.).

We invite you to attend one of our Evening or Morning Workshops.

> With best wishes,
> The Werkteater

At the first Evening Workshop the troupe played a number of single scenes, including the scene with the incurably ill child; the "Osdorf" scene, in which the widower dies; the bragging between Marja and Daria about romantic adventures; and the street interviews. After the presentation, as usual, the actors talked at length with members of the audience.

On 7 March 1974, two days after the first Evening Workshop, Shireen grouped the actors in pairs and asked each pair to make specific suggestions for constructing a solid form. The actors proposed the following ideas:

• The main setting is a parlor or sitting room in a home for old people.

• Through various transformations, we see the old people's past experiences, their unique lives.

• As in a medieval morality play, we sense that life is a journey in which exchanges with others are of central significance. As the characters realize this, they have a great deal to tell, and they can prepare for "the last supper."

• The performing space is used to present tableaux vivants that derive from personal associations with being old.

• The journey through life is symbolized by means of the Little Red Ridinghood fairy tale. Little Red Ridinghood is the young person who is constantly interrupted by society (the wolf) as she moves toward old age (the grandmother).

• The whole piece is set in a waiting room. We become aware of human reality through associations. Hearing the other residents' troubles, the residents who are waiting are freed from their own troubles.

• The performance area has two platforms: one for young people and one for old people. Each group has its own theme, and in performance they react to each other.

Given the diversity of available material, no one expected to discover an easy way to unify it. But choosing an integrating principle or process proved extremely difficult because the actors feared that any compromise would weaken the basic force of each proposed structure. Moreover, the very fact that the old people being portrayed were withdrawn and psychologically isolated created a serious problem: the first attempts to make human connections between them were awkward and forced. Helmert suggested writing a scenario based on the existing characters, but this idea was soon discarded. Peter felt that by working through an individual character, each actor could make visible anything he or she wanted to show; thus each actor could evolve a kind of plot for his or her own character. The company finally decided that during the next week, 11–15 March, the actors would not undertake any group work but would concentrate instead on trying to investigate their own stage characters more thoroughly. Shireen said that if anyone needed to play out central moments of the character's life with another actor, she would arrange it. She emphasized again that they were not to invent more but rather to work at deepening what they had already created.

Sometimes, however, the process of close examination can destroy the courage to push on and even threaten an actor's belief in his or her own powers—and that is what happened at this point. Vitality failed, and the actors went limp with frustration. The project had reached its nadir. What seemed to push the actors beyond this impasse was the experience of performing in public at the next Evening Workshops.

On 19 March 1974, patrons entering the company's Amsterdam theater in Kattengat Street for the Evening Workshop were greeted immediately by a series of tableaux vivants, so that they were led gradually into the performance and made aware that the players would not confine themselves to the playing area. The action began with a song from *Gang*, a carnival piece of medieval origins sung by three blind men. Marian Buijs described the setting that night as follows:

"Three Blind Men Are We," a beautiful three-part song, surprises the members of the audience, who have just hung up their coats there in the lower room of the Kattengat. The W.C. door opens, and there they come, each wearing dark glasses and carrying a white cane. They hold on to each other, seeking protection from the sighted world around them. On the steps [leading up to the performance hall above] they meet a frail old woman in a dark brown dress and hat. She drags a trashbag up the stairs. Only a few people [among the spectators] offer her a helping hand. Naturally she is not really old. The spectators laugh in confusion, not knowing what is expected of them. Upstairs on a little platform behind the bar sits a widow of fifty who is looking for a friend—at least that is what a sign in front of her says. The audience members take their places in an area where two tables are standing. At each table sit two men. One of the men plays with some beads; another stares at a photograph. In their activities they are quickly and progressively becoming older. In this manner they convey the essence of what is to follow.[2]

After the four Evening Workshops the actors added to the opening of the piece a song about life's ending. This song, which was taken from the performance of the first *Twilight*, briefly revealed what was to ensue. From the earlier proposal to use two platforms, the company decided to keep one small platform,

2. Marian Hofland-Buijs, "U lijkt wel een ouwe appel opa," *Toneel teatraal* 95, no. 6/7 (June–July 1974): 21–23.

about three by six feet and one step high. It stood upstage center in the playing area, against a riser at the rear. The riser, running along the wall, held a single row of chairs on which the actors sat when they were not on the little platform or the floor of the performance area. This line of people was also taken from the first *Twilight*. Nine people, one behind the other, sat as if in a train. After the song two young people, a son and a daughter, came to take two of the people to an old people's home. The ensuing parent-child dialogues occurred simultaneously, and the speeches had to be spoken in a very concentrated way, so that together they created a particular rhythm and formed a unity.

Inspired by a Dutch television piece called "Father Abraham," the actors decided to stage a final party at which each individual in the home would present for the others something important for him or her. This scene would give each the chance to convey clearly something about himself to the group. The party scene was tested on 4 April in a Morning Workshop done for working girls, and as a result it was retained and expanded.

During the actors' discussion of the 4 April presentation Marja offered the idea of showing that dying can be a wonderful event if it is experienced as a complete letting go with someone who deeply loves you. With the group's approval she developed the following scene with Yolande. In the sitting room of the old people's home, Marja, a somewhat distracted woman, comes across Yolande sitting alone in a chair. Sensing that Yolande is sick or dying, she sits beside her and begins to comfort her, combing her hair and then holding her as she vomits. Yolande dies slowly, struggling a little but finally giving in, and Marja carries her off in an embrace. When the scene was played for the whole troupe, it cast a very particular spell, and the company agreed that it had to be the concluding scene in the production.

In the Evening Workshops the actors' insecurities sometimes led them to seek support for their characterizations by imitating physical frailties, slipping into caricatures, or giving verbal explanations of activities. During one of the evaluation sessions Shireen emphasized again that they should not be concerned with playing old people but should try to find out for themselves what being old means and then attempt to reveal that.

In their efforts to reach the workshop audiences the actors were willing to go to almost any extreme. They wanted no-holds-barred communication. But their loyal public seemed largely conditioned to expect something else. Apparently they wanted the actors to reinforce their own critical views about how society treats the elderly. Just before the beginning of the third Evening Workshop, Shireen tried to dispel this erroneous expectation by announcing to the audience that the performance would not deal explicitly with the social problems surrounding old age but was intended instead to let the actors show what being old meant to them as individuals. Despite this warning from Shireen and the deeply personal energies put forth by the actors, the individual discussions between players and audience members after the performance generally grew impersonal. Most spectators immediately translated their subjective reactions into discussions about structures of society they felt ought to be changed. The company began to realize how difficult it can be to draw a spontaneous response from an audience that insists on reacting intellectually.

The Werkteater was discovering what their later experience proved: they could elicit spontaneous responses more easily from people who seldom go to the theater. Such people often give the actors details of information and experience that they can incorporate in their performances. Rense said: "Sometimes in a discussion you meet someone who approaches you personally, who doesn't put up a complicated barrier, someone who simply tells you something about himself. And then you become wiser about yourself and the work."

On the other hand, a few members of the workshop audience did recognize that the actors were trying to present, not simply old people, but the quality of individual lives in which youth and age are always present. They saw in the actors themselves young and middle-aged people who remain continually visible and present through the characters that they play. These audience members recognized that the actors were deeply concerned with capturing fundamental human experiences—isolation, loneliness, loss, and lack of power, but also yearnings for communication, play, friendship, and love. This reaction was gratifying because it fulfilled an original goal of the Werkteater: to present the characters of old people in a way that would make spectators more keenly aware of universal human experiences.

The actors reacted in a variety of ways to the Evening Workshops. Some enjoyed them more than working in private; others felt quite the opposite. But for everyone, they served to diminish the anxiety about presenting a finished product. No one feared chaos anymore. Everyone was eager to improve the production by trying out new ideas. For example, one problem lay in the audience members' failure to understand the reminiscing of the old characters, their plunges back into youthful feelings. The actors first tried putting passages of reminiscing into an atmosphere of daydreaming after the midday meal, but that did not seem to succeed. Then the performers noticed that when Rense and Helmert recited their two interwoven monologues, reacting associatively to each other, they were using their own real memories of childhood, and in the act of telling were becoming like children again. Thus when Rense tried sitting on Helmert's lap during one of his deep rememberings, the inner transformation from age to a childhood state became clear to everyone, and immediately opened the way for other characters to do similar things.

During the evaluation of the Evening Workshop on 10 April 1974, Shireen and several actors said they had sensed the growth of a cyclical form: the life of the piece opens in the morning, with hope; it progresses through the day; and as evening and the final party approach, the atmosphere seems to imply death but also has hints of birth. With this in mind they worked more on tightening up the scenes, focusing on essentials in them, and fitting the various parts into the overall structure.

The Evening Workshops had demanded not only individual clarity but also individual responsibility for the whole. The period of uncertainty, when each actor was thrown back on himself or herself and forced into greater self-discovery, lasted an unusually long time. But in the end the actors found renewed trust in their own powers and in each other. As Shireen commented: "It has been a difficult process, and we have gone through a lot of misery. But it's been worth it. The actors as individuals have achieved a lot of depth, and they have gotten past a lot of stereotypes. Perhaps the same result could have been obtained in a much shorter time, but I don't know whether it would have produced so much for each person individually."

On 19 April 1974, the Werkteater circulated the following notice in its monthly newsletter: "We have developed a new project, tentatively entitled *Twilight*. The performance dates will be May 3, 10, 15, and 17. A day of closed rehearsal with Shireen will precede each of these evening performances. Completion of the project will take place in September, after which we will play it as often as possible."

Twilight as Performance

As planned in April, the finishing of *Twilight* occurred after the summer vacation and tent-theater performances. Development of the annual tent-theater production had begun on 25 April, a week before the final workshop presentations of *Twilight*. Beginning on 18 September 1974, the actors took up work on *Twilight* again. In a ten-day period they managed to do the rough shaping and settle on a structure, which for all of its incompleteness offered the actors security.

Increasingly, each actor established a unique character that would develop during the course of the performance. Explicit reminiscences of youth were condensed, and even removed, and their content was used instead to illuminate the present state of the old characters, who thus gained lucidity and integrity. One example was Gerard Thoolen's handling of the memories of his character, van Geffen. Van Geffen, a friendly, rather silly man who had always lived alone, hears from the doctor that he may now eat anything he wants. He is delighted but also anxious, because he suspects that this means he will die soon, no matter

what he eats. For the first time after twenty years of strict diet-
ing, he sits and eats a ham sandwich, talking incessantly about
memories of convivial times at the dinner table. In reality, he is
sitting there alone because the ominous nature of his news has
prompted the other old people, including a Mrs. Walewska,
to leave the table. In this situation he recalls the happy times
around the table in his parents' home and talks about them to
the now absent Mrs. Walewska, who, he says, always reminds
him of an earlier love, though "nothing ever came of it."

Some of the actors, in fact, said they felt that they *became*
their characters while performing, so deep and intuitive were their
actions and reactions on stage. Such statements reflected the
fact that they were making greater and greater use of their own
personal feelings and attitudes. This incorporation of personal
feelings could be seen, for instance, in two of Rense's moments.
When a schoolgirl visits the old people's home and asks to hear a
bit of wisdom from an old man, Rense's character tries to think of
something high-sounding to quote, but he cannot remember the
wording. Later, as his presentation at the party, Rense's character gives a poignant explanation of what the images in Brueghel's
"Fall of Icarus" mean to him. Because this painting is one that
has deep meaning for Rense personally, his character's explanation on stage came across as absolutely genuine, a bit of hard-
won wisdom from an old man.

As the deepening process went on, the actors demanded still
tighter form. Several anecdotal elements were removed, and
eventually they dropped the opening song of the blind men. And
since their audiences now numbered more than a hundred, instead of a few dozen that participated in the first Evening Workshops, they dropped the tableaux vivants that had greeted the
first small groups of spectators. They disagreed among themselves about the quality and function of various parts of the
whole, and continued to hold opposite opinions about its anecdotal or episodic aspects. Costumes were abandoned during
the Evening Workshops, with the exception of three or four
items. And gradually some of the actors began to use their own

names instead of the fictitious ones originally assigned to the characters.

Twilight opened on 27 September 1974 and played nearly every Friday night during the autumn. On 12 February 1975, the Werkteater presented it for the first time in an old people's home. Previously groups of older people had come to the Amsterdam theater to see the play, but playing for an audience that had to remain under special care in a home was a different matter. For this performance the actors omitted the kiss between Peter and Rense, the funeral home advertisement (which in March they also dropped from regular performances), and the defecation scene with Joop and Marja. Even more important, they made everything in the piece more optimistic by several degrees: they sang whole songs instead of bits and pieces; Marja flirted a little with Peter; Joop danced with Marja; and there was more laughter, though they played the final scene with as much intensity as usual. By this time the actors were so secure, and the framework of their piece so solid, that they could alter scenes at a moment's notice and even adjust the inner moods of the whole work to match a special atmosphere.

Twilight was performed as a theater piece until May 1977. In May 1976, a German version was performed in Hamburg and televised by the Norddeutscher Rundfunk. Finally, during the 1979–80 season, the Werkteater created a special one-hour adaptation for German and Dutch television.

FIGURE 1. *Twilight*. Before the opening song.
Left to right: Herman Vinck and Joop Admiraal.

3

The Performance of *Twilight*

Text, Actors' Commentary, and Notes

The Werkteater is located in a renovated factory building in Amsterdam. Performances at this time were given in an upstairs room, with seats provided for about 150 spectators; its rectangular playing area, a bare floor about forty feet wide and fifteen feet deep. Members of the audience sat around three sides of this space, on a level with the actors, sometimes nearly touching them. This was the setup for *Twilight:* across the rear of the playing area ran a long, narrow, three-foot-high platform supporting a single row of eight chairs, facing stage left. Right in front of this was a lower platform, a foot and a half high and three by six feet: it served as a step-up for the actors and was used by the actors when they made their presentations in the party scene. A table with two chairs stood at both the left and the right downstage areas (Figs. 1 and 2). Only general lighting was employed.

The dress used by the actors for the performance of 15 November 1974 was as follows. Helmert: a dark blue sweatshirt and pants. Daria: dark blouse, slacks, and red handbag. Marja: light blue terrycloth bathrobe over shirt and slacks. Yolande: at beginning, a dark dressing gown with a pattern; then an almost ankle-length black dress and thick woolen socks. Anna: shirt and jeans. The actors played in clothing that they would also wear off-stage, with the exceptions of Daria's handbag, Marja's bathrobe, Yolande's dress, and perhaps the vests of the men.

Normally the actors would use their own names in performance. There are some exceptions here, but three months after this text was recorded, Peter Faber dropped "Stijlstra" in favor of "Faber." During the 1974–75 season Anna Korterink was an apprentice with the Werkteater. After that time other company members, including Shireen Strooker (who served as the stimulator on the project, a directorial function), played the directress and sometimes guests played the schoolgirl.

On the lefthand pages facing each page of the play text are actors' comments about their feelings and their work in creating and performing *Twilight*. Where the comments pertain to specific lines in the text, those lines are preceded by an asterisk. These comments, and those throughout the book, were collected during the spring of 1975 from tape-recorded interviews with the actors and from their written notes to the author (see sources listed at the end of this chapter).

Performance
Dynamics
and the
Amsterdam
Werkteater

———

FIGURE 2. *Twilight*. Helmert Woudenberg (standing)
sings in the party scene. Actors seated,
left to right: Herman Vinck, Rense Royaards,
Joop Admiraal, Daria Mohr, Peter Faber,
Yolande Bertsch, and Gerard Thoolen.

Twilight

CAST

Joop Admiraal	Mr. van Beusekom (except in second scene)
Peter Faber	Mr. Stijlstra
Rense Royaards	
Gerard Thoolen	Mr. Vincent van Geffen
Herman Vinck	
Helmert Woudenberg	
Yolande Bertsch	Mrs. Walewska
Marja Kok	
Anna Korterink	Directress of the home; schoolgirl
Daria Mohr	Mrs. van Draden

PLACE: A home for older people

TIME: The present

STIMULATOR FOR THE PROJECT: Shireen Strooker

TEXT: Tape-recorded at the Werkteater, Amsterdam, November 15, 1974. Transcribed by Emmy Koobs. Translated by Dunbar H. Ogden.

Actors'
Comments
_____

Joop: As people come in and take their seats, I walk slowly onto the stage. After I sit down, I don't get out of my chair again. I'm supposed to concern myself with the audience. Doesn't work. Sit still, smoke a cigarette in a "stupid way," not inhaling much but enjoying the smoke. Paying attention to my breathing helps keep me quiet. I keep thinking, "You should do something," but I don't know what. I look at people's shoes. Everyone has different shoes. Now I'm quieter, and look at people without interest. Everyone has a different face. I avoid looking at people I know; it makes me unsure. I try to pay attention to all the different faces that are nothing to me (Beusekom), with whom I don't want to talk. I'm afraid I'll lose the character of Beusekom. Peter does talk with the audience, very well. Herman too. Herman talks with me, and I put him down. Herman doesn't get anything from me—but then from Beusekom no one gets anything.

Rense: The audience is close. You can touch them. Some of them give you a hand, a coin. I used to keep my eyes closed, but I don't do that anymore. It makes me too closed off. We sing a number of rounds. When we get into a good mood, sometimes we also mix in other songs.

Peter: I sit at the table and look at the people in the front row and beyond them. I feel that I am sitting here for the last time this evening, so openly in contact with the audience. To me the song is a kind of farewell, a contrast with what is certainly going to come: to be put away in an old people's home and become isolated.

Marja: I wrote "It is all past" together with Joop; we took it from the early version of *Twilight*.

Herman and Joop enter and eventually sit at the table stage right. Peter eventually sits behind the table stage left. They smoke, talk to themselves, occasionally to each other and to members of the audience. Walk about rather stiffly.

From offstage right three blind men wearing dark glasses shuffle on in single file, each with a hand on the shoulder of the one in front: Helmert, Rense, Gerard. They are singing a somber, medieval-sounding song about blind men. Eventually they come to stand on the rear platform, face front. At the end of the song they take off the glasses.

Four girls prance on—Yolande, Marja, Anna, Daria—and stand, each with a hand on her hip, in front of the upstage men. The girls stamp their feet and, together with the former blind men, break into a bright, new song. Herman, Joop, and Peter join in.

ENSEMBLE (*sings*)

    It is all past,
    We haven't yet begun,
    This is the end,
    But where then have I been?
    It's come this far,
    Our business isn't done,
    You must get out,
    But was I ever in?

ENSEMBLE MEN (*sing*)

    Mother, it's famous I want to be.
    A little more coffee while I sit.
    I really want to be a star.
    'Til I get moving, just wait a bit.

As the singing continues, the downstage men, one and then another, stand up, address lines such as the following to the audience, and eventually sit down.

*HERMAN, PETER, JOOP (*variously, speaking*)

I haven't thought about it. I have things to do. It isn't closing time yet. Have you got a cigarette? (*Etc.*)

ENSEMBLE (*sings*)

    It is all past,
    We haven't yet begun,
    This is the end,
    But where then have I been?

Daria: The objective of this scene is to contrast young people with old people. The old people are "tiresome and conceited"; you make a little fun of them, feel young and independent. I always feel pretty self-assured—who'll mess with me? I look at the audience. It's a daring start, unexpected and with a lot of noise. It always relieves me because it's not heavy and pretentious. It's not a tightly directed ensemble, and I like that. You feel everyone's presence and you know for sure that the play has begun.

Actors'
Comments
———

Joop: Using a hoarse voice when singing isn't necessary, but I'm always doing that. I'm afraid to seem young. Also I twitch at my mouth, and shouldn't do that. I'm stuck on making faces.

Joop: In calling out kinds of food, I have a sort of alphabetical list in my head to keep me from hesitating. When I fall back and sit on the floor, am I dead? I don't know—I freeze.

*ENSEMBLE WOMEN (*sing*)
>Said always: God, I don't want to.
>Wish I were dead. Help me, mother.
>Now that you're about to die,
>Will you climb up out of the gutter?

VOICE FROM ENSEMBLE (*speaks*)
>One more round.

ANOTHER VOICE FROM ENSEMBLE (*speaks*)
>And everybody!

ENSEMBLE (*sings*)
>It is all past,
>We haven't yet begun,
>This is the end,
>But where then have I been?
>It's come this far,
>Our business isn't done,
>You must get out,
>But was I ever in?

*ENSEMBLE (*sings a new song, the girls sing first and third lines*)
>I want croquettes with lots of spinach,
>Chicken, pheasant, and a hare,
>'Til now I haven't got my fill,
>I'd love a glass of wine, aged rare.

>*As the singing continues, Herman, Peter, and Joop get up and move for-
>ward. Each speaks separate names of food to the audience. The volume
>increases, then decreases as each of the three finally moves upstage, sinks
>down at the feet of the ensemble, and remains motionless.*

*HERMAN, PETER, JOOP (*variously, speaking*)
>Beefsteak tartar. Mashed potatoes. Scrambled eggs. Fried
>haddock. Sour herring. A pork chop with mustard. Beans
>and bacon. French fries with mayonnaise. Thick pea soup.
>Fresh steamed kale. Meatballs. (*Etc.*)

>*Herman, Peter, Joop—each has sprawled on the floor in a partially up-
>right position, his back against the platform, frozen, stopped mumbling.*

ENSEMBLE (*sings, now in close harmony*)
>It is all past,
>We haven't yet begun,
>This is the end,
>But where then have I been?

Daria: When the song is finished, I immediately let all the tension drop, and I go and sit on a chair and move into a different mood. That's very important, not to get stuck.

Marja: I use the waiting here in order to concentrate myself on the performance. I always tell myself that I have to play four scenes and each of them has to be different.

Joop: I am thinking here about my own mother. I have often had conversations like this with her, and I know all about this situation. This scene is difficult because we speak simultaneously, something we usually try to avoid. It works sometimes—makes beautiful rhythms and still expresses the misery—but it's difficult!

Actors' Comments
———

Peter: As I sit and wait, I hope for a surprise, so that here, and often during the play, my eyes begin to fill with tears. I'm surprised and happy when I hear my son. I look at him and feel terribly proud of the big fellow standing in front of me who's doing so well. I try to get him to come and sit next to me and talk about the past. I keep saying, "What a fine boy you are." Every performance the text varies between Herman and me.

Daria: Here, for a few seconds, I think of my grandmother. She was always busy thinking about her gloves, her hats, her powder, that sort of thing. She was very well until grandfather died; then she went to the old people's home and two months later she died. In playing this, I feel like I'm a small, inquisitive little woman, a bit timorous, with a little "bird's head" and rather staccato movements. In fact, I don't play much; I don't start anything, at least when it goes well, and I don't think about being old. The longer it takes before Joop comes to pick me up, the better. As soon as he speaks to me, I look at him; we all do that. Herman also comes to pick up Peter, and the two dialogues intertwine. It's important to react to each other in a musical way. I hardly understand what the other two are saying. When they stop and only Joop and I are speaking, Joop genuinely moves me as he tries to persuade me to go with him, and I cling to all the familiar little things at home. I know this has a lot to do with my own attachment to things. My objective here is to postpone the awful moment of leaving, to invent ways to escape.

*Silence. All sit in the upstage row of chairs, except Herman and Joop, who
stand far right and left. Yolande, Marja, Daria become older women.
Anna exits.*
Simultaneously, Joop talks with Daria and Herman talks with Peter.

* JOOP (*standing left, to Daria*)
Mother, I'm here.

HERMAN (*standing right, to Peter*)
So. Dad, are you ready? Are you coming?

* PETER (*turning to Herman*)
To do what, my son?

JOOP
We have to go. We're leaving now . . .

DARIA (*to Joop*)
No. No. I can't leave things like they are now.

HERMAN
Dad, you have to comb your hair and put on your coat.
What's the matter? The taxi is waiting outside. We're leav-
ing now.

DARIA
Yes, but all my things. The suitcases . . .

HERMAN
Hurry up, dad. The taxi . . .

JOOP
Then take that one suitcase with you, OK?

HERMAN
But dad.

JOOP
Now, take that suitcase along, and the rest we'll . . . Two
bags? Isn't that a little too much?

DARIA
And those letters. I still have to go through them.

HERMAN
Look, what did we decide about the parrot? Dad. We can't do
that.

PETER
Oh, that'll be all right.

JOOP
I'll go ahead and carry that suitcase. OK? Hurry up a little.

* DARIA
I don't have my gloves.

Actors'
Comments
——

Daria: I ask directions from people in the audience. Is it left
or right? The sun is shining, and that makes it a lot better. People
in the audience often say that they don't know the way either. I feel

JOOP

I'm going on ahead.

HERMAN

You have to now. We've telephoned.

PETER

No, but . . .

HERMAN

They're waiting for us. We have to be there in half an hour.
(*Exits right.*)

DARIA

No. Come back tomorrow.

JOOP

We can't do that. We must go now.

DARIA

No.

JOOP

Come on.

DARIA

Those letters. I have to go through them. Otherwise . . .

JOOP

No. We were going to leave them here. Know what, I'll take
the suitcase downstairs.

DARIA

I have forgotten something.

JOOP

And when I come back, I want you to have your coat and hat
on. Then you come with me, mother. We really have to go.

DARIA

No, I just can't.

JOOP

Yes.

DARIA

I can't leave things like they are now.

JOOP

I'll take the suitcase down and when I come back, then we'll
leave together. (*Exits left.*)

*All of the actors get up from their seats; slowly walk about and over to the
audience. They make easy, friendly remarks to each other, to themselves,
and to members of the audience: "Hello." "How pretty you look." "Now*

aimless and lost. So I leave rather quickly at the side. This scene gives me a good starting point, so I can settle my thoughts and concentrate.

Peter: My mind begins to wander. I know now that I have to go to an old people's home, but I want to avoid the realization by thinking about other things. At this moment I think what a fine son my boy is. I carried him when a baby, washed him, comforted him, taught him to hit back, helped him at school, showed him how to impress girls, and so on. Now he has arranged all this for me. I try to think I'm going on a visit—a beautiful initiative on my part. But then I stand still, and feel, think, and say: "I'm not going." I'm still talking to myself so I'm completely amazed by the sudden appearance of the directress.

Actors'
Comments
———

Peter: I feel like a kindergartner who's scared to death on his first day of school, and I try at the same time to make a good impression on this cute young woman.

Peter: I protest, I want to give my own opinion to the directress. In my next lines, when I mention a fellow who smelled, I want to let her know that there are people to whom I am superior. Then, when I mention bright colors, I'm despairing but trying to be optimistic. I'm slowly forgetting the presence of the directress. When I look at the empty chair, I think, "My predecessor sat there, curious." Then I try to adapt myself to the situation by making a joke, and I sit down.

let's see what it's all about." "You have to keep an eye on things, you know." "Marvelous." "Lots of initiative, too." "Marvelous initiative." All leave the playing area.

* PETER (*enters from stage left*)

I know the way here like the back of my hand. I don't have to ask directions from anybody. I can do everything. It has nothing to do with your age. I know exactly where I am and where I'm going. Great plan. Well meant. I'll act as if I like the place. Very friendly. Bit bare. Lot of green. And nice faces. (*Becoming angry.*) But I'm not going to fall into this trap. I'm going back. I'll write a note. I still have some good connections. I'm not going to fall into this trap. (*Walking away.*) In their pretty little plan.

ANNA (*enters from right*)

Good morning. Are you Mr. Stijlstra? I'm Mrs. Kortering, the directress here.

PETER (*stopping*)

Oh, I think that's . . .

ANNA (*shaking hands*)

Good morning, Mr. Stijlstra. You're right on time. We'd agreed on ten o'clock.

* PETER (*half to himself*)

Cute directress.

ANNA (*laughs*)

But you haven't a single . . . Is it cold outside? And you're not wearing a coat. Aren't your children with you? Well, come on in. It's nice and warm in here. Just leave your suitcase out there. We'll take care of that. It's warm in here. We'll get you a cup of coffee. Now. It'll be handiest if I show you how to find your way around here. When you go straight through there, you'll find the bathrooms. A bit farther to the left in the hall is a billiard table. You can use it every evening from seven to nine. For the chest beside your bed, I'll give you your own key. You may keep it yourself. And each month a nurse will check to see if everything's all right. That's OK, isn't it.

* PETER

I'd rather not.

———

Daria: My intention is to appear deeply injured, short-changed, and really too good for this world. I'm full of self-pity, but I'm terribly proud that I don't let anyone see it. I think, "I'll get my chance." I've chosen this self-pitying attitude quite consciously, because I believe it explains why elderly people are often so diffi-cult to approach and shut off so many possibilities for contact. Someone who demands a lot of attention won't get it very often. Maybe I'm afraid of becoming like that myself.

ANNA

Well, you'd better talk it over with her.

Peter protests.

ANNA (*crisply*)

Especially—we will expect you to change your underwear every week and to bring us the laundry.

PETER

One fellow in my building, he smelled, I tell you.

ANNA (*laughs*)

Yes. That's why. Now I'll take you over to the lounge. By the way. Do you have your burial and insurance papers with you? I'll put them away for you in the safe.

PETER

Bright colors here, too.

ANNA

Yes. Every evening you can watch TV. Only, we're the ones who control the buttons. That's OK, isn't it. (*Indicating chair at stage left table.*) And this chair, Mr. Stijlstra, recently vacated . . . is your chair.

PETER

What was wrong with the person?

ANNA

Nothing serious. Have a good time. (*Exits left.*)

PETER (*sitting, to himself*)

If he didn't have drop-sy!

During the last lines, Daria, clutching her red handbag, has taken a seat at the stage right table. Her lips are pursed.

MARJA (*entering from right, loudly to Daria*)

So. Come on over to me, girl. All of a sudden I see you sitting there. No. (*Seeing Peter.*)

Hey, hey, who stinks here so?

The little man in the radio.

(*Sits opposite Daria.*) Hey. How thin you're getting. If I blow, you'll just topple. You're so thin. At first you were . . . Oh, you're getting such a beak. You know what you look like? Like a sparrow. O, birdie, birdie, birdie, birdie, birdie, peep, peep, peep. . . .

Peter: During Marja's lines, I'm constantly trying to catch the attention of the ladies. When Marja accidentally looks in my direction, I stand up and say firmly, "Stijlstra." When Marja says, "Keep quiet," I'm offended, but I put up with it and sit back down.

Actors'
Comments

―――

Peter: I see another chance to make contact and just shoot out the last part of my name, to get it in quickly.

Daria: This line is the turning point. When we created the scene, we thought about how these women, as close friends, would share the kind of fantasies they got from reading romantic novels. Because I claim the gardener for myself, I break up the friendship, because that's against the rules of the game. This lays the foundation for our interaction—very important for us as actors, though not important for the audience members. What is important here is the theme of jealousy between women.

Peter: I'm sitting here listening, and when Daria says she's going to see the gardener, and says how nice he is, I imagine that I'm the gardener and I get very emotional.

Marja: In this scene I'm afraid at first to interrupt Daria too much, but as I listen to her, interrupting doesn't seem to matter and becomes natural. Here I always had a theater-school frustration: now I've got to play something, a transition, being hurt, etc. Recently that's become easier. I just let it happen. I just listen to her, and then it happens by itself.

* PETER (*laughing, introducing himself*)
> Peter Stijlstra.

MARJA (*turning to Peter*)
> I'll see to you in a minute. Keep quiet. (*To Daria.*) Hey, listen sparrow; a new one. Birdie, a new one. Hey, you've lost your smile. Can't you smile? Sparrow. It doesn't suit you. It doesn't suit you when you look so sour, girl. Come on. Tell me. What's the matter? What is it now? Are you mad at me? 'Cause of yesterday? 'Cause yesterday I said you were a twit? Love, you're so sour. But I mean, I don't really think you're a twit. You're not a twit at all. You're just, just, just, just—You're just like that. My friend. I'm proud of my friend. You do it with style. With style.

* PETER
> . . . stra. (*Laughs.*)

MARJA (*to Peter*)
> Are you the funniest one at home, huh? (*To Daria.*) Listen, shall we tease him? You know, like we did yesterday. Hey, let's go tease him, come on. Big girl. Christ, girl, look what a day! Think what all could happen today!

* DARIA
> Well, I have to go now. I have an engagement—with the gardener.

MARJA
> No.

DARIA
> I think he's already waiting for me.

MARJA
> No.

DARIA
> At the same place as yesterday.

* MARJA
> No, the gardener is with my friend today. You know that very well.

DARIA
> He said he was going with me today to the greenhouses.

MARJA
> With you?

Actors'
Comments

———

Daria: In my enthusiastic fantasy I overstep the line by thinking up this tale about Marja. I've been thoroughly enjoying my
lies. Now I flounder in my words, and do something in my pants—
everything runs, and I'm lost, totally dependent on this very Marja,
and I beg her for help that she refuses, angered and distressed as
she is. I whine and feel shame and am totally helpless.

DARIA

It's so lovely and warm in there. Then he shows me every-thing: the roses, the marguerites, the buttercups. (*Laughs.*) Then he takes hold of me. And he massages my neck and shoulders.

MARJA

Aren't you ashamed?

DARIA

Then we go outside.

MARJA

Aren't you ashamed?

DARIA

He said we'd stay outside a long time today.

MARJA

How can you tell such lies?

DARIA

And we won't come home for lunch. I've already told them. We're going to the park.

MARJA

What are you going to do there?

DARIA

We always sit on a bench. He brings all kinds of goodies with him: chocolate. He puts them in my mouth, one by one.

MARJA

You don't dare look me in the eye when you . . . Because it's a lie. Every word's a lie.

DARIA

I've put on my special walking shoes. Afterwards we go to the shed. We have to go through the dark. Through the darkness. Through the underbrush. He takes me with him, and the door opens. It squeaks a little. It's so dark, inside. Then he lights the oil lamp.

MARJA

And.

* DARIA

And then he says, "Mrs. van Draden, may I take your coat?" He hangs it up. And then he fixes a place and he says, "Shall we?" For the floor is covered with rose petals. So we lie down. It's beautiful. And then . . . (*Suddenly hysterical.*) and

Peter: I get up and say my name charmingly, so they'll like me. I get frightened at Daria's predicament, and hesitate. Then slowly, carefully, I walk toward this bent-over woman and look around to see if there isn't some help for her. Shall I help her? But how? Suddenly I begin to sing and rock her back and forth by very gently pushing her on the back. When I shake her hand, I'm thinking she's a nice little lady, seems willing, maybe something can develop between us.

Marja: What Daria and I are supposed to be doing with Peter remains uncertain, but I guess it's all right because it's where we meet Peter for the first time. We'll stick to the scene because it gives us a feeling of "What's happening now?"

then he tells me that you slipped in a puddle and that you had a big, ugly stain on your skirt. And he doesn't tell it once, he tells it twice!

MARJA

You shut up.

DARIA (*breaks into a laughing and coughing fit, doubles forward*)

Can you call somebody? Please, can you call somebody? It's coming.

MARJA

Eh? You pour all that on me?

DARIA

Just ring the bell for me, just ring.

MARJA

Come on.

DARIA

Give me that cloth over there.

MARJA (*to herself*)

No.

DARIA (*letting go in her panties*)

I can't hold it any longer. Help me.

Daria sobs occasionally, but calms down during the remainder of the scene.

MARJA

I have to go. I have a date. With the gardener.

DARIA (*sobbing*)

Help me, a little.

* PETER (*has tried not to intrude, but becomes sympathetic and gets up*)

Stijlstra.

DARIA

Help.

* MARJA (*to Peter*)

Stijlstra! What kind of a name is Stijlstra, man. You're just sitting there prying and spying. Your ears are so big you can hear it all, can't you. Damned creep. You're that type, aren't you. One of them. Are you green with envy now? God help me. This house is filling up with your type. (*Sits in upstage row.*)

PETER (*starts to sing a familiar-sounding Dutch song and moves toward Daria*)

Daria: Peter shows sympathy and curiosity, and comes over to me. I'm a sad and filthy little heap sitting there. I try to pull myself together as best I can, to keep up appearances, and to act as if I'm meeting him with my best dress on. I behave as if I don't have anything to do with the whole business.

Peter: It's my own feeling that this action occurs a month later. I try to get van Beusekom to laugh, and above all I try to make an impression, brag, etc. When I'm doing this, I feel myself physically off balance, dizzy. When I say "turn on the news," I march intrusively over to van Beusekom and say the next line right at him. Then I walk right back to van Geffen and Herman for an affirmation of how funny I am. When I say, "I know another real good one, Beus," I'm trying to show them that I've been around, seen a lot of places.

Joop: When I enter, I'm uncertain, and irritated by the presence of Peter. I don't want to listen, but I hear everything that follows. I'm annoyed. I can't handle it, and get up with the line about queers.

And we'll never let each other go.
And we'll never let each other go.
And we'll never let each other go.

* DARIA (*dries her eyes*)

How do you do. (*Shakes hands.*) Mr. Stijlstra. (*Gets up.*) Somebody will be here right away to clean it up. Don't worry about
it. Good-bye. Good-bye. Mr. Stijlstra. (*Sits in upstage row.*)

Joop crosses and sits at table left. Then Gerard and Herman sit at table right.

* PETER (*to Gerard and Herman, who laugh throughout*)

The only one around here who already begins to stink in the
morning is van Beusekom. (*Laughs.*) Van Beusekom didn't expect that, did he? (*Laughs.*) Humor, so early in the morning.
(*Laughs, makes noises.*) Hey, boys. What do you say, eh? Funny,
huh, a real good one, eh Beus?

* JOOP (*always very dry, never laughs*)

Yeah.

PETER

You don't even have to turn on the news. You get it here. It
used to stand in my way; now it hangs in my way. Hey, yeah!
Funny, huh, boys? It used to stand in my way; now it hangs
in my way! (*Laughs.*) I know another real good one, Beus.
When it's so warm in here, like when the central heating is
up a little too high and the humidifier isn't filled, huh, and it
can get a lot hotter, Beus . . .

GERARD

Not possible.

PETER

And a big, wide plain, where they all swarm around . . .
with little white houses. And those fat, brown bastards at-
tacking from the front. And from behind . . . with their
spears. They were going to stick me, Beus. Stick me, Beus.
They screamed—Hooonda. Hooonda. Hooonda. And I kind
of step aside, Beus, I step like this, with my right foot in a
little cradle. . . . (*Laughs.*) Beus, I'd love a juicy piece. Get
that, boys? Meat. (*Laughs.*) Beus is a vegetarian.

HERMAN

Come on, Beus. Come sit over here.

Peter: At "a juicy piece," I'm an entertainer enjoying his own double entendre: "juicy piece" means juicy woman. At "meat," I feel success; this one's right on target. But then I see that Beus doesn't react at all to my stories, and I can't stand that; it makes me insecure. So I use the butcher story to demonstrate strength, daring, and potency.

Joop: The line about the queers isn't good. Too aggressive. I can see it in the audience. Everyone knows that I'm a queer, so they think "What is this?" Could be different. I could be someone who wants to be a homosexual but doesn't dare, and so I challenge other men that I suspect are like me.

Actors'
Comments
_____

Peter: At Joop's line about queers, I think "Try me," but I'm getting fearful and uncertain. I feel pumped dry. Feverishly I start dragging in proofs that I absolutely couldn't be a queer. Van Geffen and Herman think that I am. I try to make them listen, but they go away. I'm left behind alone. I get excited and say, "I beat the hell out of a guy" to the people entering with the chair, and get back the response "All that rubbish." At that I leave. I want to flee, to go outside, to go I don't know where.

Rense: What happens here is that Helmert causes a kind of softening in me: I can trust him with something. When we sink into talking about our own memories, it isn't rational communication, it's pure association. But that doesn't matter. It relieves some of our loneliness. We're sharing something. I'm basing this part on my own memories of Bergen and Schoorl. I lived there, so I never had to travel there with my parents. It's not the train trip, it's more the atmosphere of the polder and the dunes I'm using. I've tried to make my memories seem like those of a city dweller, a bit lyrical and literary—static, perhaps. Helmert's memories are much more those of someone who has worked there—they are more to the point, less on the periphery. He hasn't measured everything for its beauty. He's felt everything with his hands. Helmert always pro-

*PETER

I say to the butcher, "Butcher, now give me a real nice schnitzel." And the butcher says, "What did you say, sir?" I say, "A real nice schnitzel." And the butcher says, "Come around behind." And I run right into the p-i-t-c-h black. Get it, boys? You know where I . . .

*JOOP

Say, you know what I absolutely hate? Queers.

*PETER

I've got such a pile of letters from women. S-u-c-h a pile. And do you know what the women write me? They write: "When I know you're coming, my legs won't stay together." How about that, van Geffen? "When I hear the bell, I start to sweat." Such a pile of letters from women. I also had a woman, and I'd just helped her across the street. . . . And wood. Hauled wood, too. All the women that swarmed around me.

HERMAN

He doesn't mean it like that.

PETER

And I beat the hell out of a guy once. Stuck my knife in him.

RENSE (*entering*)

All that rubbish. We can't stand it.

Joop, Herman, Gerard go to upstage row, sit.

From off left, Rense pushes Helmert on stage, in an easy chair on casters. Peter tries in vain to engage them in conversation, then also sits in the upstage row.

*RENSE

Let's go sit in the sunshine. So. Here's your spot. Look how the sun's shining. Every time spring comes I get that same high feeling I used to have when I went with my parents to that little village by the dunes. We got on the train in Amsterdam, and we sang all the way.

(*Sings.*)

Look for sun beams,
They are so fine,
For a ray of sunshine
That must be mine.

And then in Alkmaar we changed to a little steam train.

vides me with associations that let me continue my trip from Amsterdam to the sea—a trip from now back into my childhood.

Helmert: My foster father was an old farmer, and I did live on a farm. The idea about a man who didn't like trains is something I made up. I imagined a farmer who gets angry at trains because they remind him of big cities and things. The next memory, the laborers jumping over the ditch—that's real. I really saw that.

Helmert: The woman biting off the rat's head, that's only partly made up. When I lived on the farm, there was a boy about twelve or thirteen who got frogs out of the ditch, and for a quarter or a dime he'd bite the frog's head off and throw the frog away. And I remember rats very well. When I was very young, six I think, I would play in the hay with a girl, and one day we saw two little eyes in there and heard something hissing. We ran off and called my brother. My brother said, "Oh, there's a rat," and took the pitchfork and jumped into the hay. He got the rat and slammed it all over the farmyard. When we went to look at it, it was dead. My real father and mother died when I was very young, and I grew up in a farm family. My foster parents loved me very much and I loved them, but I was a strange duck in that pond. And they were very primitive, so there were a lot of fights at home. I can remember very grotesque fights.

HELMERT (*now sitting stage center*)

My father didn't like trains at all. He said they didn't exist. And so when we boys found a paper or a magazine with a picture of a train, we took it to him and said, "Dad, this is a train!" Then he'd get fiery red, and he'd stand up, snatch the paper from the table, rush to the door, turn around and say, "Traitors!" Then he'd go to the outhouse and wipe his ass with it.

RENSE (*standing beside Helmert's chair*)

And then you rode. Under a radiant sky, you rode along the North Holland Canal. And then at the windmill of Koedijk you turned into the polder [field reclaimed from the sea]. And it was like a god's hand had strewn the pastures full of flowers. And the birds were in the air. And the ditches were full of duckweed and ducks.

* HELMERT

The polder ditches were fifteen feet wide or more. And there were men from Brabant—hired hands—and they were working for us. They would kick off their wooden shoes, take a run, and jump clear over that ditch! Fifteen feet or more! What men! God!

RENSE

And then you arrived at that little station under the trees. And Roland Holst stood there with his walking stick. And then you got off the train and you smelled the sea air, mixed with the steam from the locomotive.

* HELMERT

And there was a woman with the Brabant people—that was one tough woman. She could fight and work like the men. And if you gave her a quarter, with her bare hands she'd catch a rat from the threshing floor and bite its head off! Aagh, like a chunk of bread.

RENSE

And then we hiked through the dunes to the sea. And there was that day when we saw a rabbit, leaping and dodging. We ran, ran, ran after it, and I don't know how it happened, but then . . .

HELMERT

Saturday the children had their bath. They were all rounded up. Their clothes were taken off. And then, like puppies

Rense: At the end I'm moved by self-pity. I see that little boy before me who still has to live out a whole life. I feel sorry for him because he will still do his best, even through all of the pain—and pleasure. And why? In order to end up as an old man who sits by the window and gets tears in his eyes when springtime returns, because the springtime is as inaccessible as his lost childhood. When Helmert takes me on his lap, I feel like that little boy again who fell down and is comforted.

Yolande: Here, I've just come from the doctor. I go through three moods. The first is rebellion. What must become clear is that I'm someone who tries to hold everything together, who refuses to

they were dumped into the tub. They sloshed, and they splashed, and they laughed. That was so much fun. . . .

RENSE

Then I tripped. I tripped.

HELMERT

The other day a little boy fell off the roof.

*RENSE

And a trickle ran down my chin, and great red drops dripped on my white suit.

HELMERT

O little boy, come here. Children should play. They mustn't be sick. Come over here, little friend, come here, my little boy. My little man. (*Takes Rense by the hand, then onto his knee.*) And when they're sick, then you keep them busy all day long. Then you play one game after the other, and you never get tired, because they have to get better, the little ones. So they can play again.

My little boy, O little boy, my little friend. You even smell sick. Your father isn't here. Your mother isn't here. But I'm with you. (*Tears run down Rense's cheeks.*) You'll get well. Then you can play again. One game after the other. (*Bounces Rense up and down, more vigorously at each line of the child's chant.*)

So goes the master's horse, and the master's horse
goes so.
And so goes the lady's horse, and the lady's horse
goes so.
And so goes the farmer's horse, and the farmer's horse
goes so!

Helmert slumps a little to one side. Rense stands up and begins to push the chair up left.

RENSE (*affectionately*)

Come. Let's go eat. Let's go eat. You're getting fat, my friend. Your legs are getting thick. Let's have some dinner.

Eventually Rense sits in the upstage row.

*YOLANDE (*entering from off right; shouting toward off right simultaneously with Rense's last lines*)

Nooo. Nooo. Don't do it. Stupid, every one of you. Dumb.

subject herself to anything. The second is determination to show that I can manage things, because I don't want to be a burden to anyone; this ends when I say, "That's written down." Then I start to give way and get a little desperate. When van Beusekom comes in, I pull myself together and get rather aggressive. He's clearly the kind of man I don't like at all. He irritates me no end.

Actors'
Comments

———

Joop: Van Beusekom is aggressive toward the doctor. He takes it out on Yolande, or anyone, but never on the doctor. He's cowardly, always bitching. I saw people like that when my father and my mother were in the hospital, and when I've had operations myself. I hate people like that. When van Beusekom is bitching and bragging, I'm afraid of slipping into a type. I hear myself talk. I think, "There you go play-acting again, just when you have to do your best." But toward the end of the scene I slip right in, I don't think anymore, I just do it—nice feeling.

The whole lot. Do it to other people. But not to me. (*Sits at right table.*)

Joop sits at left table; Yolande continues speaking front.

They don't know a thing. Stupid, all of them. What they have learned, *that* they know. But they know nothing about my body. That's what *I* know. *I* know what's wrong with me, and I won't lie down. (*Shouts.*) Do you all hear? I will not lie down. Injecting me, giving me pills: it goes on and on. I won't let myself be poisoned. When I'm dead, OK, then they can have me. Then I'll go to the royal anatomical laboratory. I'll go. That's written down in black and white. (*Drums her fingers on the table.*) And that's my right. It's my right to decide what they do with my body. They can have my kidneys and the corneas of my eyes. They can have it all. But only then. What are they meddling for? I'm not doing anything. Never complain. I have suitcases full of photos, and I've never troubled anybody with them. You'll never hear me . . .

*JOOP

A fathead, that's him, a fathead. Dr. Korteweg, *he* was a good doctor. This one is a fathead. I said, "X-rays should be made. Then you'll see." He says, "Are you tough?" Well, I can handle pain. I've stood the worst pains. I'm tough enough. I've had kidney stones, and that's one of the worst kinds of pain. Scientifically proven, one of the worst kinds of pain. I've withstood it.

YOLANDE

I once had a baby.

JOOP

That's something completely different. That's natural. That's easy.

YOLANDE

It was a very big baby, Mr. van Beusekom. It was a breech birth.

JOOP

A stone is unnatural. That, that's crystals, and they go through a tiny little channel. Understand now?

YOLANDE

That was in a barrack, in the tropics, Mr. van Beusekom.

Daria: Here, I have just seen the doctor. I think he's wonderful because he is so attentive—with him at least you can exchange an intelligent word. And he is so handsome, learned, friendly. You really get support from him because he knows how you feel without your having to say anything. I feel both self-pity and pleasure at having someone affirm how difficult life is for you and how the others don't recognize that at all and misunderstand you. Mrs. van Draden begins to cry when she thinks about that but also laughs because someone has recognized it. She is so self-absorbed she doesn't even hear the negative remarks by Yolande and Joop.

Yolande: When Daria comes in, I show that I don't like her a bit either.

Joop: This works well, taking away from Daria. Make everything kaput. Van Beusekom can certainly handle Daria's happiness.

JOOP

And then you get . . . a big tube shoved through you—

YOLANDE

Just shut up, Mr. van Beusekom!

JOOP

And then you have to be tough, you know. 'Cause otherwise you'll pass out.

Daria enters from off right; Joop continues.

I said to them . . .

* DARIA (*standing at right chair*)

"How strong you are, Mrs. van Draden," he says to me. "Someone who has gone through so much suffering and so much grief . . . and good things. And then, still to be so strong." (*Cries.*)

JOOP

Who?

*YOLANDE

She deserves a medal.

DARIA

I didn't ask for it at all, but all at once he says . . .

YOLANDE

Legion of Honor.

JOOP

The doctor?

DARIA

"Mrs. van Draden," he says, "What a beautiful age you're at."

YOLANDE

Yes. Yes.

*JOOP

He just doesn't know what to say.

DARIA

Still, it's good that somebody says things like that to you, because around here you'd never hear that, things like that.

JOOP

That you aren't all that . . .

DARIA (*sitting at right table*)

Around here you'd never hear things like that.

Actors'
Comments

Peter: I say this while I'm putting down the plates with bread on them. No one reacts to it. What I mean is that I'm going to make an end of it, of my life.

YOLANDE

No. Only at the Queen's palace.

Peter, who has brought on four plates of food, stands. Daria, Yolande, Joop eat during the following scene.

Gerard steps down from the upstage row. He eats toward the end of the scene.

GERARD (*buoyant, laughing*)

Everything. Now I can eat everything.

DARIA

"Mrs. van Draden," he says . . .

GERARD

Yes. Now I can eat everything. I can eat everything again, the doctor said so. Yes. I've just come from the doctor. He says, "Mr. van Geffen, you can eat anything you want. Anything. Yes, eat anything you like." I can eat anything at all I want. Now I can have everything.

*PETER

I went and got a recipe for euthanasia.

His remark unnoticed, Peter returns to upstage row.

GERARD

Now I can have everything. (*Sits at table left.*) Twenty years I've been on a diet. Mrs. van Draden, you know that. You know that. Twenty years. Nothing to eat. Tried all kinds of things, huh. (*Laughs.*) I can eat anything. Name me something. Just name me something, Beus.

JOOP

Blood pudding.

GERARD

Blood pudding, I can have it. I can eat it all. I've gotten a little thinner, but that doesn't matter, he said. I can eat everything now, he said. I asked if the medicines . . . The medicines, I don't have to take them anymore. (*To Yolande.*) Just look at those, Mrs. Walewska, the white ones with the crack in the middle. You can have them. You can have them all. I still have a whole bottle. I don't have to take them anymore. No. For me it's . . . Just start right at the beginning again. (*Laughs.*)

JOOP

Bon appétit. Yeah.

Actors'
Comments
———

Gerard: My father was very corpulent, a very big man, and he loved life very much. Before he died, people thought he just had stomach flu, but it got worse and after only three days in the hospital he was gone. Afterwards it was clear that his stomach and intestines were already dead when he entered. But what I play is not my father; it's only a reflection of him in me, in the way I see things. The way I lived, I missed the experience of loving everything. My mother was sick very often and needed the children to give her lots of attention. I see my character, van Geffen, as somebody who wants to love life but can't embrace it—there's a stone in his heart all the time, and he's only talking about a longing. When he knows the end is near, he still has this feeling, "There must be some moment that can be nice." That's why I say it's just like Christmas—I can be reborn, and start again, and do everything.

Yolande: I like Gerard. I haven't had much contact with him, but he doesn't irritate me. When it becomes clear to me that he is dying, I'm confronted with my own illness again. I eat, but I also want to be alone again.

Joop: I figure that van Geffen has cancer, and that stuns me. I can't put him down; it's too serious. I feel a kind of compassion because cancer is one thing he just can't do anything about. But I can't sit at the table with a dead man. I've got to eat and get out.

Daria: As Mrs. van Draden I've been identifying with van Geffen emotionally because he's so happy, also because of that doctor, but now I realize that they have given up on him. Quietly I start eating, but it doesn't taste good anymore. Inside I become very quiet and small, fearful because something like that could happen to me. When I leave and wish him "All the best," I have mixed feelings of sympathy and distaste.

*GERARD

It's like Christmas, eh? Before, I never could join in. I was in all kinds of clubs, and when they had their annual picnic, I never could join in. That's awful, eh, to have to pass up everything: you can't have this and you can't have that. But not now. Now I can have it all. (*Laughs.*) I'm really happy, you hear. Yes, yes. A good time here with everybody, a good time. Finally I can join in. At least that's what I feel like, a good time. Yes. And in the evening I can go to the fridge, and if . . . Sure, go to the head nurse. I can do it all. Yes. Good, eh. I'm so happy.

*YOLANDE (*going to the upstage row*)

Good luck, eh Vincent.

GERARD

Yeah. (*Laughs.*) And alcohol too. I can drink whatever I want. Yes. (*To Joop.*) What'd you say?

*JOOP

I didn't say anything.

GERARD

Oh, no? I'm so happy. Really happy. (*Laughs.*) Enjoying it. Yes. Tomorrow I'm going straight out and buy a sack of nuts.

*DARIA (*going to the upstage row, pauses by Gerard, kindly*)

All the best.

GERARD

Yeah. Yeah. Ah. So. Yes. Now we can join in again, with everybody.

JOOP

Yes.

GERARD

Cheese, too. I can have cheese, too.

JOOP

Ahuh . . . Ahuh . . . Yes . . . (*Gerard eats.*) Well, I'll be off.

GERARD

Yes.

JOOP

I've finished.

GERARD

I'm so happy that I . . .

Marja: In the scene that comes here, we used an idea from Margaret Mead's *Male and Female*. She says children who are toilet trained too quickly experience their sexuality as holding back and then letting go, just the way they urinate. With children who are not toilet trained quickly, their sexuality is much more relaxed—they play with it and experience it. I don't think the audience sees this in it, but that doesn't matter. For us, this scene is about love and intimacy.

JOOP (*crossing to downstage right*)

Sure. I'm glad for you, too. All the best.

Throughout the following scene Gerard remains seated at the left table, staring absently at his plate.

As Joop crosses, Marja stands at the upstage row and arranges a spit-curl in the middle of her forehead.

MARJA (*to Joop*)

Are you waiting for me? (*Comes over to Joop.*) It made your ears turn red, I see. (*Puts her arms around him.*) First, rub for a while. Like this. Let's go outside, what do you say. Let's go out in the fresh air.

JOOP

Yeah. In the fresh air.

* MARJA (*taking Joop's arm*)

Here, give me your arm.

They begin crossing toward downstage left.

Let's go out in the fresh air. Oooooh. How marvelous it is outside. Oh, I could shout out loud. Smell the cold air, so crisp. It's really cold. Marvelous. Look at the trees. How beautiful. Those trees.

JOOP

Here?

MARJA

Oh, they are so beautiful, those trees. You know what those are? They're pussy willows. They're so soft, the pussy willows. You couldn't break them open, even if you wanted to—I've tried. They're so soft.

JOOP

Yeah.

MARJA

Here? No, there's a mud puddle. (*Leading Joop by the hand around upstage left, behind left table, to stage center.*) Come on, let's go find a nice place. Here. Look.

JOOP

Here's some moss.

MARJA

Leaves, everywhere, red and brown. Autumn colors. OK? Yes?

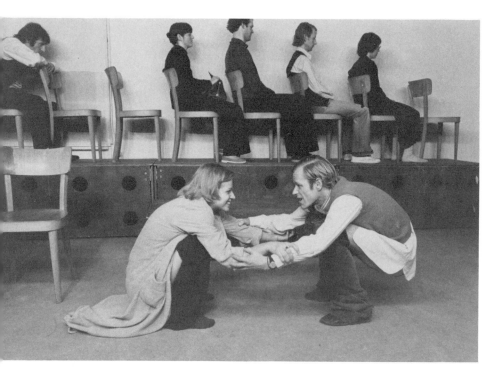

FIGURE 3. Marja Kok and Joop Admiraal.

JOOP *(facing Marja)*
  Yes? You want to, don't you?

MARJA *(unbuttons her slacks)*
  If we do it . . . If we do it together. So beautiful in the still-
  ness. All the birds.

JOOP *(unzipping his trousers)*
  Yes.

MARJA
  Do you feel it? *(Pulls up her slacks.)* I can't do it.

JOOP
  Why not?

MARJA
  Can't you just say something nice to me? *(Joop touches her face.)*
  So.

JOOP
  Here we go.

MARJA
  And we'll do it so, so nice and calm together, eh, so we'll feel
  it from each other, and so on.

JOOP
  Yes.

MARJA
  And you hold it back a little, so . . .

  *During the following dialogue they push their trousers to their ankles,
  leaving underwear on. With her left hand, Marja grasps Joop's right wrist.
  As they squat down, facing each other, she also grasps his left wrist. And
  Joop holds her wrists.*

MARJA
  Just sit down, so it'll last a long time.

JOOP
  Yeah.

MARJA
  Hey. Good. May I . . .? Are you comfortable?

JOOP
  Yeah.

MARJA
  Are you comfortable?

JOOP
  Let it come.

Actors'
Comments

———

MARJA
Yes.
JOOP
Go ahead.
MARJA
Together. OK? Do you feel how marvelous that is, with each other? Feel it now?
JOOP
Is it coming?
MARJA
Yes. Is it coming?
JOOP
Yeah.
MARJA
Yes. With me too.
JOOP
Let it come.
MARJA
Hold it—push it.
JOOP
Yeah. Yeah.
MARJA
Push it, push it.
JOOP
Yeah. Let it come. Let it come.
MARJA
Yeah. Push it. Yes. It's coming. It's coming.
JOOP
Aagh.
MARJA (*with her right hand, picks out a leaf, wipes herself*)
What a nice hard one you have. So firm. I haven't had one like that in years. With me it's always so loose.

Joop struggles to stand up; cannot.

Wait a minute. Wait a minute.
JOOP
Yeah. Just give me a little push, will you.
MARJA (*lets go of Joop, gets up, moves over behind him*)
I'm coming. Wait.

Actors'
Comments
———

Marja: I always have trouble here in letting this scene come to
an end.

JOOP (*supporting himself with his left hand on the floor, helpless*)
Just give me a hand.

MARJA
Yes, I'm coming to help you.

JOOP
Just get my trousers. . . .

MARJA
Here. I have a nice leaf to wipe you with.

JOOP
You don't need to wipe me.

MARJA
Sure I do.

JOOP
No. It isn't necessary. I'll pinch it off.

MARJA
So, did you do it? Oh, look.

JOOP
You don't have to wipe me.

MARJA (*stooping, wiping him*)
Ah, sure. That's nice. You're so clean.

JOOP
If you don't help, I'll fall over.

MARJA
You're not brown at all. You're so clean.

JOOP
Yeah.

* MARJA (*pulls Joop upright again; helps to zip up his trousers*)
Just give them to me sometime, your pants. I'll give them a
nice washing. Come on, then. . . . (*Looking at the ground.*) Hey.
Yours is all red. See it?

JOOP
From the beets.

MARJA
Mine's completely sloppy.

JOOP
You ought to go see the doctor. Are you coming?

Pause. They face each other, upstage center.

MARJA
Couldn't you just say something nice to me?

Joop: Marja is disarming; she doesn't do any play-acting. I'd like to be able to do it that way too, but I can't. Marja doesn't play-act, she *is*. She forces me to do it better, *to be*. She lets it happen. For example, when I say something nice, like "little girl," tears come into her eyes. This scene is touching because of her.

Gerard: When I was a boy, every Sunday afternoon we had the opera on the radio. My father would lie on the couch with his paper over his face, and everybody had to be silent—it was an un-written law. He would listen with tears in his eyes. I've missed being in a family, all the everyday things you learn from people. I think that's why I remember those Sunday afternoons as moments of real happiness—enjoying things like a duck walking over the table. Yes, it really happened. We had a duck. Nine children, and I was the youngest. When I play this scene, I really prepare. I try to create a base for van Geffen's happiness. It's tragic: he knows his life is over, but he still tries to make plans to see what could happen; and it's also a last chance to offer love to Mrs. Walewska [Yolande]— to really find out if he can say to somebody, "I love you."

Actors'
Comments
——

Gerard: When van Geffen says, "I used to know someone with black hair, but nothing ever came of it"—that's true. And the story about the sand pit, that's also part of a real happening. It was during the war I think; the boy who was in the pit was saved. But what I thought about was van Geffen eating, and suddenly having his mouth too full, like the boy in the sand. He wants to cry out for help, but then he's blocked. I think that's an image for van Geffen: at the moment he feels what freedom is, what you really could do, his mouth is so full that he can't say anything. And that's the moment when he realizes that it's all over for him.

*JOOP (*stiffly touches her face*)

Little girl. Huh? We have to get back now.

Marja and Joop go to sit in the upstage row.

*GERARD (*still sitting at left table, hums "Va', pensiero," the slave chorus from Verdi's opera* Nabucco, *and then speaks toward a chair at the table stage left*)

You know that song, don't you, Mrs. Walewska? It was always on the radio on Sunday afternoon. Remember it? Always opera, always opera, wasn't there? So familiar. Cozy, at meal-time. All ten of us sat 'round the table. Yes. I always thought that was so cozy. No, it isn't like that anymore. Everybody talks and . . . Don't you know. Always on Sunday. There were twenty of us at times. Oh, sure, we'd have twenty people at the table. A little bread in the ground meat made a larger piece, but . . . Yes, yes, yes. I'm so glad that I can join in again, because I always thought it was so cozy. We had a white duckling. (*Gets up and puts a chair from right table beside him.*) Come over and sit by me, Mrs. Walewska. That's cozy, isn't it. Eh? Now I can eat everything again. I can join in with all the others. Yes, so . . . Oh, I wanted to tell you about the white duckling. That little white duck, we used to let him run around among the dishes. (*Laughs.*) Oh, yes.

Everybody left home, everybody. Yes. I was the only one remaining. Yes. Well. I could deal with it very well, you know, with being alone. Oh, yes, yes, yes. You have, I think you have such beautiful black hair. I think it's very beautiful. I haven't ever said that to you, but that's what I think. I used to know someone with black hair, but nothing ever came of it. No. (*Laughs.*) We dug a hole six feet deep, Mrs. Walewska, yes, six feet deep. And then whole troops sat in it. And all of a sudden one of the sides caved in. Completely caved in. (*Laughs.*) They were there under the sand, the children. Yes. (*Cries.*) Completely under the sand. Yeah, sure. I could hear them calling. Through the sand I could hear them calling. They were trying to call for help, but they couldn't. They tried to, but their mouths were full of sand. (*Breaks down crying, and eventually returns to the upstage row.*)

Peter and Rense step down from the upstage row and begin clearing up the dishes. Peter is up center; Rense starts out down left. At each of the following bits of song, one actor sings and the other joins in with a few

Actors'
Comments
—— .

Rense: When we started on *Twilight*, Peter and I wanted to make something that had to do with "love." We chose an office situation: two people who work together day in and day out, and never admit one thing—their love for each other. What began as a long improvisation has been reduced to this scene with the little songs, that ends with a kiss.

Peter: This scene evolved from some improvisations that Rense and I did about sex. We improvised from this situation: two men who work together in an office harbor secret longings and feelings about the world, each other, themselves. Under a lot of tension, they kept these feelings hidden: they were taboo. But during a telephone conversation, or as one of them handed something to the other, a contact developed that transformed their situation, so that they would feel, for example, like a boy and a girl at a dance. We've dropped all of this, and preserved only the mutual need for contact, warmth, intimacy.

Peter: In the scene now, I stand behind Rense, who is clearing up. I have followed him in spite of myself: perhaps I can make contact with him. I feel drawn toward him, probably because he is so different. I know that at times he sings old songs, so I sing a few lines, wait, and sure enough it happens—Rense joins in with the next lines. This continues while Rense hands me the plates and keeps coming closer to me. At the end we stand right in front of each other, and our heads keep coming closer together. We kiss each other and then stand there looking around blankly like a

words or by humming. Neither knows a whole song. Gradually Rense comes over until he stands face to face with Peter. [The songs are familiar in Holland.]

PETER (*up center, sings*)
> Look for sun beams,
> They are so fine,
> For a ray of sunshine
> That must be mine.

*RENSE (*downstage left, starts to sing another song*)
> Although my tire's a little flat,
> My baby, you're not fat,
> So hop up on the back,
> So hop up on the back,
> So hop up on the back.

*PETER (*sings another song*)
> Tonia, Tonia
> Three times all around, and hopsasa
> Tonia, Tonia
> Up above my old cot
> There you saw my portrait.
> Tonia, Tonia . . .

RENSE (*sings another song*)
> When the bell of Arnemuiden

They hum together.

PETER (*sings another song*)
> And the two of us, we're better as a pair
> For alone it is so lonely everywhere. . . .

RENSE (*with his face very close to Peter's, sings another song*)
> Look in my eyes and see the tiny people,
> Look then at the dimple in my chin. . . .

*PETER (*sings another song*)
> Oh, how pretty you are,
> Oh, how pretty you are.
> So pretty a thing I haven't seen in years,
> So pretty, so pretty.
> Oh, how pretty you are.

As usual, Rense has joined in. The song dies away. Silence. They look at each other. They hold plates. Slowly their lips meet. Pause.

couple of chimpanzees. Herman and others enter, and we break the silence with "Jingle Bells." We feel caught, ashamed, and we separate. For me personally, this is the only scene in the play where I went through a kind of evolutionary process together with some-one else right from the beginning, in the content as well as in the form. In all other scenes both content and form still change con-stantly. But here only organic reactions, attitudes, and words come to the surface—from out of my experience with an old sentimental seeking for love and security.

Actors'
Comments
———

Herman: The story about the crucifix—it's sort of a defense of a way of life, which is perhaps a personal thing, now, for me. I've always been too busy, working very hard. I studied painting and sculpture in Brussels until I was twenty-three years old. Then I got an important job as a designer, and after one year I was head of the design department in a firm that made industrial packing. Then in theatrical companies I was acting, I was assistant director, I was director, I made designs for the sets and costumes. I was always busy, busy, busy. Now, for the first time in almost fourteen years, I begin to realize why: in personal matters I don't function all that well. Perhaps that explains a little bit of the aggression I show here.

Joop, then Herman and Gerard step down from the upstage row. Peter, embarrassed, sings. Rense quickly gives Peter his plates, moves down-stage, and joins in the song.

PETER (*sings*)

> Jingle bells, jingle bells,
> Jingle all the way,
> Oh . . .
> Jingle bells, jingle bells,
> Jingle all the way,
> Oh what . . .
> Jingle bells, jingle bells,
> Jingle all the way. . . .

Peter goes off left, and eventually returns to the upstage row. Helmert also sits in upstage row. Herman, Rense, and Gerard sit at the table right; Joop at the table left. During much of the scene, Rense nods off.

GERARD

Once a little boy came to our door and presented us with a bill. It said: "Water leak investigated, but not found—twenty-five guilders."

Laughter.

*HERMAN

I know what you think. I know your kind. I've had to deal with them all my life. Yeah. You look down on people who use their hands. I could make anything. Anything, anything. Golden hands. (*Rising, becoming increasingly agitated.*) They always said so. Golden hands. With wood, with tile, with iron. And when I came here, I didn't sit around on my ass all day, like you all. I used my hands. I wanted to do something. I made a crucifix out of 8,742 matchsticks. (*Showing its size.*) Such a crucifix. Craftsmanship. Real craftsmanship.

GERARD

Nice.

HERMAN

And fourteen days later, do you know where I found it? In the trash can.

JOOP

Of course. What's the use of such a thing, of a crucifix?

Rense: Throughout the schoolgirl's visit, I feel like a spectator.
I'm self-absorbed. I dream, doze off, fall asleep.

ANNA (*entering briskly from off left, carrying a school bag*)

Good afternoon, gentlemen. I'm Annamarie, from the high school over there.

With the exception of Joop, the men respond enthusiastically: "Hello," "Good afternoon," etc.

GERARD

Are you in nursing?

ANNA

No. We're doing a project.

HERMAN

A what?

GERARD

A project?

ANNA

A kind of research.

HERMAN

A what?

ANNA

It's about old people.

JOOP

Good idea.

ANNA

Yes.

HERMAN

You're at precisely the right address.

* RENSE (*rises*)

    I have as many memories as leaves
    rustle on the trees, as whispering reeds
    along the streams, as birds . . .
    (*Sits.*)

GERARD (*to Anna*)

He's forgotten.

Pause.

ANNA

Well, our principal, she phoned the directress here, and she said I ought to talk with the person here who has the least visitors.

Actors'
Comments

Joop: Van Beusekom doesn't really get it. He can't put her down. When she talks about visits, he starts to understand. When he hears that his name is the only one on the list, he is nice in his own way because he has been chosen for something and not the others. But later on, when she asks him, "Why are you here?" he turns off.

GERARD

Oh, yes.

ANNA (*fumbling for her notebook*)

I've written down the name.

HERMAN

Say. I know you. I know your face. You ride your bike past here nearly every morning—on a sort of high black bike, eh?

ANNA

Yes.

HERMAN

Oh, yes. I know you.

JOOP

On the bicycle. With all the other girls, of course.

ANNA

Yes. (*Reads.*) "Mr. van Beusekoms."

JOOP

That's me. Without the "s." "kom."

ANNA

Oh. May I sit here with you?

*JOOP

You've come to visit me?

ANNA (*sitting*)

Yes. Because we're doing a project. Because, maybe we could do something to improve conditions.

Gerard and Herman nod and laugh.

JOOP

A project.

ANNA

Yes.

JOOP

Sooo. A project.

ANNA

Yes. (*Pause.*) Should I come back a little later?

JOOP

Yes. Yes. Later, yes. OK.

HERMAN

That's bright.

Herman: When we were improvising the first time, Shireen told us to react to the physical presence of a young person, so I reacted immediately to her figure, how she was built. That's a bit personal, a bit Belgian or Flemish. [Herman is Belgian.] The Flemish way of saying you love someone, or even that it's nice to see them, always seems rather aggressive to a stranger. All the joking in Flemish is very aggressive, but it's a sign of love, of warmth, and it's totally different from what the Dutch do. Totally different. They can't say, "I love you." They'll almost make a curse out of it. Here, in this scene, I'm trying to say that it's a very important thing to be young, to be alive. I'm trying to express what my father and grand-father could never say. Perhaps even more, I'm saying, "Don't live like I did, because I've failed to live." That's what's behind my anger in the speech a little later, the one that ends, "Print that in the paper."

ANNA
Tomorrow morning, should I . . .
HERMAN
Say. Is it easy to ride your bike with such tight pants?
ANNA
Oh, sure.
JOOP
It's the fashion. She can't help it.
ANNA (*to Joop*)
How long have you been here?
JOOP
Since sixty-nine.
* HERMAN
You have a good figure. Know what you ought to do? In the morning when you wake up, before you eat breakfast, you should go outside and wash in ice-cold water.
JOOP
She's embarrassed, eh? Five years and six months, nearly seven months.
HERMAN
Is your hair really that color?
ANNA
No, that's henna.
HERMAN
Ah. What? Henna?
ANNA
It's a plant. You can make powder from it.
GERARD
She has a plant in her hair.
HERMAN
The hair is the ornament of a lady.
GERARD
Really pretty.
ANNA (*searching in her bag*)
No. No.

Herman stands behind Anna's chair.

JOOP
Looking at your watch, child?

FIGURE 4. "Print that in the paper."
Herman Vinck to Anna Korterink.

ANNA
 No. I just have to find the list of questions.

JOOP
 Oh, yes.

ANNA (*opening her notebook*)
 Now . . .

JOOP
 Now the following question . . .

ANNA
 Why are you here?

JOOP (*pauses*)
 That's no question.

HERMAN
 Come on, give the girl an answer.

JOOP (*gets up, crosses, sits in Herman's chair, right*)
 You do it then, if you know so much. (*Mumbling.*) That's no conversation.

   Herman sits in Joop's chair.

ANNA (*to Herman*)
 May I ask you . . .

JOOP
 Sure.

ANNA (*to Herman*)
 How long have you been here?

JOOP
 Very long. Already before me.

ANNA (*to Herman*)
 OK. Do you like the food here?

GERARD
 Yes. Fine.

HERMAN
 Can't complain. Why do you have to know all this stuff?

ANNA
 It's for school, for the project.

HERMAN
 For school? What do they have to do with it, at school?

ANNA
 I just made a list that I thought maybe I could use when
 I . . .

Gerard: There's a sort of strength in young people—an open, right-away sort of speaking and saying things—and I think here van Geffen feels that. He's longing to start again, to be someone who's entering the world, studying. I myself always have that same feeling with younger people. They need to explore situations. That's why I love young people and don't want to see them get closed off too early.

HERMAN

You shouldn't use it in school. Use it in the newspaper. Use it in the newspaper. On the front page, they ought to write it. (*Angry, pounding the table as he talks.*) On the TV screen, they ought to show it: how they've just abandoned me here. My own daughter. My own son-in-law. I haven't seen her in a year. I just went home. There I stood at the streetcorner. My grandson came up, and do you know what he asked? "Are you looking for somebody, mister?"

Loud laughter.

Print that in the paper.

ANNA (*has gotten up*)

Yeah.

*GERARD

You should come over beside me, eh? Come sit here. (*Slides Anna's chair across to his.*) I'll just get your chair. (*Anna sits; Gerard takes her hand.*) Good project. Come on. So. So. Yes. Yes. I'm happy, you know. I can eat everything now.

ANNA

What do you do all day long?

GERARD

Huh?

ANNA

Billiards?

GERARD

Billiards, too. Yes.

ANNA

Do you read?

GERARD

Read, yes, a little, eh?

ANNA

Handicrafts, making nice things?

GERARD

Well, that would mess the place up too much, eh? You could, all right, but they don't. They do . . .

JOOP

Everything for appearances.

GERARD

Anybody that wants to. You can choose.

Actors'
Comments

———

Marja: Almost always I feel dreadful doubt and awful fear when I have to do this scene, but after the first sentence, that goes away. The scene has been shortened a lot. I concentrate on opening myself out toward the audience. Sometimes I forget that this has to come from within myself, and then, when I talk directly to the audience members, they become defensive. It's a fantastic exercise. Everybody should do it. This is what you really should strive for in acting: not to say that you played it well, or badly, but that something else happened that you couldn't escape. The audience members, unconsciously, always react in the right way, so you learn an awful lot from them.

ANNA
What kind of advice would you give, as an older person to a young girl?

Pause.

GERARD
Oh, I wouldn't know.

ANNA (*to Rense*)
And you?

JOOP (*to Rense, dozing*)
She's asking you something. What kind of advice you have. As an old man. For that girl.

RENSE
. . . the interview, eh?

GERARD
He just talks to himself.

ANNA
Oh, I mustn't forget—how do you divide up your day?

JOOP
They divide it up *for* us, like a pie. In little pieces.

RENSE (*rising, solemnly*)
I . . . wait a moment. Life . . . it is advice . . . life offers the opportunity to exist. . . .

Anna exits left, shaking hands, nodding good-byes.

JOOP (*to Anna*)
Write that down.

Herman exits left. Joop, Rense, and Gerard sit in the upstage row, as Marja steps downstage center and addresses the audience.

*MARJA (*boldly, buoyantly*)
Hey, boys. It's hot in here. Am I ever warm. My head, my head, it's going to bust open, hey. Oh, it's hot in here. Aren't you getting hot? Now I'm dripping. I'm telling you. From top to bottom. Oh yes, I have a fever. Fever: 105 degrees. Pretty serious, huh? But let's get on with it. I don't want to talk about that, 'cause I've had so much in my life. I have here a . . . (*Points to underarm.*) I had a lump here—sooo, such a lump here. They did something totally new—came with a kind of pistol and shot it out of there. And if it comes back there.

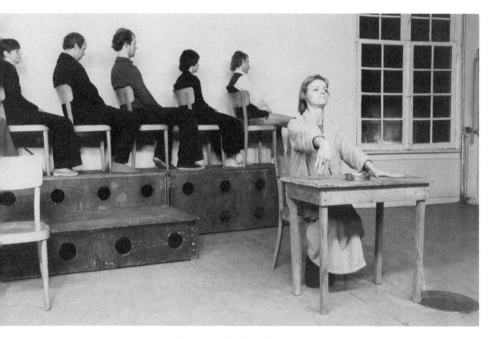

FIGURE 5. Marja Kok delivers the news.

(*Laughs.*) Then you don't have to understand what I mean anymore, get it? But that's not the point now. I'm only telling you that I'm sick because they came and stood around my bed.

Four of them. Came to grab me. Came to grab me. They say, "Now, come on out." Because they need me. (*Taps her chest.*) They need me. And do you know why? 'Cause they like to laugh. They want a good laugh. Look, I'll explain it to you. Tonight they're going to have a party and then everybody has to do something. Lots of fun. Everybody, they do something, so it's lots of fun. Out of me they get a big laugh. Sometimes they almost choke, laughing. Really true. Yes. (*Lines here are some of her many spontaneous reactions to audience laughter.*) That does you good, eh? Yeah. I can't help it. When I come on, people just start to laugh. Shall I show you? What a shame you can't see me tonight at the party. You'd laugh. . . . (*Laughs.*) Oh. Look, when I come on, on the stage, people just start to laugh. I act like I don't notice anything and go and sit down. (*Sits at left table, facing audience.*)
Feel the tension in the room. Do nothing. Suddenly I say, ka-pow: "Good evening, ladies and gentlemen, here is the news." Hey? Hey? Get it? That's unexpected. I think that's unexpected. You usually see that on the TV, and then you see me. Boom. The news. You don't expect that. Then I say to them: "The Pyrenees. Early this morning, at the top of the Pyrenees, a cyclist failed to observe the road sign *No Through Traffic.*" Get it? Can you understand me over there? Should I speak louder?

AUDIENCE

No.

MARJA

Now that's good. Did you get that one, too? You'd better let me see that you get it. You didn't crack a smile. Come on, boys. (*Pointing to other audience members.*) Look, they're bustin' a gut. That's what it's all about. Really. Sometimes I get scared. I'm really afraid. I think: girl, listen, if you're funny, too funny, that's a big risk. 'Cause some of them never got up. I saw somebody fall out of his chair, pop, just like that. And a bit later, another one, puff. On the ground. Then they came to get them with an ambulance. Out they go. I just went on.

Actors'
Comments
———

Herman: We made several scenes about people from the outside world coming inside to this other world. A visit or something.
We also had scenes where the older people of the home were re-
belling and breaking out, trying to build a new life. Well, one day
Shireen [the stimulator] gave me the directive to make a visit
to Helmert as my father. Why we're still doing it, I don't know.
Helmert gets very violent in it, and I get very afraid. And it's still

And I think: they like it, they're asking for it. We have to laugh, ladies and gentlemen. I'll go on. One more. One more. This one: "Italy. This morning a party of tourists climbing the volcano Vesuvius was caught in a stream of hot lava." Huh? Listen, that could be. That could be. It happened. Well, let's not argue about it. My point is—(*Pointing behind her.*) They laugh 'cause they think: Those people shouldn't have gone on vacation.

Get it? Hey? Did you get it? Feel it? Does that grab you? (*Gesturing behind her.*) They can't ever go on vacation, so they're happy about the others' bad luck. Listen. Happy about others' bad luck—if somebody else can go on vacation and then, paf, he's out. That's humor. That, that is humor. Come on, admit it—when somebody else has an accident. Look, look at me. When somebody falls down the stairs, I bust a gut. Really. Admit it. Admit it. What's healthier than a good laugh, eh? That's the best medicine, I always say. Now I'll give you this one, because *I* think it's funny: "Brussels. Late this afternoon, as delegates sat on the Common Market Advisory Board, it splintered into factions." Hey? That one's unique. That's just damned good. You know, it's such a pity that they don't put things like that in the news. That's why I announce it. It has a meaning, a deeper meaning. Listen. Do you get it? The delegates sit on the board and, paf, it splinters. Get it? (*Rises.*) That's got to do with language.

At this point, Herman enters from left, pushing Helmert in an easy chair on casters. Herman's opening phrases are interspersed among Marja's last lines.

That's a question of language. But here's what's important for me. I really wanted you to laugh tonight. So you don't think we're all so . . . Not at all. When we laugh . . . with us you can laugh. (*Exits right.*)

*HERMAN (*pushing Helmert along*)

Soooo. Hello, father. Now this . . . you didn't expect to see me, did you. Want to go out and sit in the sun, father? You look good, father. They take good care of you. Your hair's combed, and . . .

HELMERT (*absently*)

Yeah.

going on like that. The last time we did it I said to Shireen, it's terrible to do this, terrible, because I'm really afraid of Helmert. And why the slapping has to be there, I don't know. I only know that it reminds me very much of my relation with my own father, because I was very afraid of him. He didn't slap me very often, but once I got a slap in my face. He wasn't at home very often, but my mother was always saying, "Wait 'til your father gets home." I was eight or nine years old. Also, during my first marriage I didn't have much money, and my father helped me some. Then my marriage broke up and I couldn't pay him back. He kept mentioning it year after year, and I still think he's never forgiven me.

Actors'
Comments
―――――

HERMAN
Now you see that it really isn't so bad.
HELMERT
Ah. Yeah. Yeah.

They are downstage center.

HERMAN
Well, what do you say? Here I am.
HELMERT
Yeah. Exactly.
HERMAN
I simply left work—so I could see you.
HELMERT
Well, well.
HERMAN
Yes. I thought, high time to make a visit.
HELMERT
Ah.
HERMAN
Yes. Hilde's watching the shop, so I can . . . You look good, father, really.
HELMERT
That's what they all say.
HERMAN
And you feel well, too?
HELMERT
Very.
HERMAN
Hilde sends you her love.
HELMERT
Naturally. Well, well.
HERMAN
Do you know that Jan, that not a day goes by that Jan doesn't talk about his granddad.
HELMERT
Ah.
HERMAN
And he says, "A kiss for granddad."
HELMERT
Ah. Well, well. Nice.

Actors'
Comments
———

HERMAN

Friendly place, here, eh?

HELMERT

Oh, yeah.

HERMAN

Have you heard anything from Henk?

HELMERT

Tomorrow.

HERMAN

Actually I wanted to talk over a few things with you, father.

HELMERT

Ah. OK.

HERMAN

Look. I'm very happy with the business. I'm not complaining, or anything, and I've carried on with it. Well. I can't complain. But this is a difficult period.

HELMERT

Yeah.

HERMAN

You know that yourself, very well. You watch TV, don't you.

HELMERT

Oh, sure.

HERMAN

I'm having a few difficulties, father.

HELMERT (*suddenly angry*)

Now, get out. Get out of here.

HERMAN

But you understand? I mean, at the moment I have some debts, and then I thought, I'll just go and have a talk with father.

HELMERT

Well, well.

HERMAN

I wanted, I wanted . . . Yes, Henk, he manages everything just great. I thought, the ten thousand guilders. Henk didn't want to do it, and I carried on. Well, I can't complain, but it's . . . But that ten thousand guilders is stuck in the bank, just sitting there earning nothing, so I wanted to ask you if I couldn't use it.

Herman: By the end of the scene, it's all over. I'm not thinking about Helmert's being dead, but our relationship is finished. It's awful. I feel total helplessness, not being able to relate. There's complete misunderstanding here, in the whole scene. Personally, I'm asking things about myself, and about my relation with my father. Sometimes I think I hate him, really, but most of the time I guess I can't help loving him.

Helmert: In my first scene, the reminiscences with Rense, my text is always the same; it's quite formed and tightened. But in this scene with Herman I'm determined to keep it loose, to change it all the time. So between the two scenes, when I sit quietly for a long time at the wall there, I always prepare myself for it differently. And Herman knows that. He's prepared to do different things. For example, on last Thursday night I tried thinking that the old man knows he is dying, and that he's preparing himself for that by trying to see everything, place everything, name everything that is coming. He wants to have a clear mind, to have everything balanced and in focus, but he's still a bit afraid that death could come suddenly and catch him unprepared. So in the performance, I'm quite relaxed, just seeing things in the room and keeping my balance. When Herman comes to get me, and starts talking about all kinds of things, it's not important to me whether he's my son or not. What's important is that he's a disturbance, he's upsetting the balance I'm trying to keep. [This effort reaches its extreme in Helmert's final speech, "I hold fast that glass."] In my own life, like when I'm at home in bed, I try to think about what it will be like for me to die, but when in the theater I play that I'm dying, it's

HELMERT (*looks hard at Herman*)

Is your father dead? Who are you, anyway?

HERMAN

Are we going to make jokes, father?

HELMERT

No! What an ugly face you have. Unbelievable, how disgusting it is. I've been looking at it, sure, but . . . (*Shouts.*) Spare me, just spare me, boy. What is the point?

HERMAN

The point is that you never liked me, huh, father?

HELMERT (*shouts, tries to hit Herman*)

Aaah. I . . .

*HERMAN

I'll never visit you again, father. You better know that.

HELMERT

No. Shut up.

HERMAN

Father, I came to ask you for help.

Helmert shouts and hits Herman.

I came to ask you to help me, father.

*HELMERT (*shouting, flailing, trying to hit Herman*)

And when somebody had to give a talk, and a rule had to be put down on paper, then they weren't at home, because they couldn't do that. But they could go to the whores. Go on. Go and check on your sister.

HERMAN

Father, that was all a long time ago. Yes. If you don't want to, OK. Me you can't help, huh? Just . . .

Helmert shouts, hits out again.

I'll go and get something for you. Be right back. (*Exits right; eventually to the upstage row.*)

During the following speech, Helmert grasps the arms of his chair and pushes himself up, with great force holding himself, still in a sitting position, above the seat of the chair. He becomes louder and louder.

HELMERT

I hold fast that glass. The room is full. It's a quiet room. I hold fast that glass. "What are you doing?" I say, "I hold fast

not the same. I can't reach that personal level because of the figure
I play, I think. So the setting in order is more personal than the
dying afterwards.

For yesterday's performance I prepared myself differently. I
told myself, "When Herman comes, I know him. I know he's my
son, but I'm very angry with him. I lived with him and his wife but
then he sent me here, so I hate him in a kind of way." So when
Herman comes and starts talking and then asking for money, I pretend that I'm not in my senses. I say, "Oh, look there, there's a
chicken," or "Oh, here comes a car." Always at first there's a kind of
conversation between us and then I get angry and strike out at
him. Sometimes I don't actually hit him. Anyway, yesterday when
the right moment came, after there had been enough conversation, I suddenly recognized him and said rude things, very rude
things. I could say them because I knew it was the last time I'd see
him, because I knew I had to die.

Gerard: Playing "The Crossing" is sort of what a clown might
do—in a moment of extremity, burst into playing something that's
both overtragical and overgay, music from the bottom of the heart
and music of celebration. I think van Geffen feels these extremes.
In the party scene I think he wants to make a sort of cry for understanding, or send a message. For me, the music is a way of saying,
"Really listen to me, because this is where I am now." It's a sort of
last postcard, with every word on it that you wanted to say.

Rense: In the party scene I chose "The Fall of Icarus" because
I associate that painting with complete solitude: someone has an
accident, disappears, and life pays no attention. It also seemed in
line with my character (and maybe with myself) to draw conclu-
sions more from paintings and books than from life itself.

Peter: Here [as Mr. Stijlstra] I'm thinking, "What a beautiful
presence Rense has, what a well-read person he is," and wonder-
ing if he's still thinking about me. When he finishes his story, I find
it wonderful. In fact, throughout the remainder of the party I feel
as happy as a child, identifying with everything intensely. So I applaud dutifully, even at the wrong times [as at the end of Joop's
act], because when you like something, you're supposed to show it.

that glass." She says, "You don't have anything in your hands."
I say, "No. I hold it with my eyes." A strong glass. I hold fast
that glass. The whole room full of animals and women that I
haven't seen in a long time. And everything rose, rose up
high, up high through the walls. I hold fast that glass. Oh, I
hold fast that glass. I hold fast that glass. I hold fast that
glass. I hold fast that glass. I don't know anybody anymore,
not my children. I hold fast that glass . . . ahh . . . broken.
(*Sinks back into the chair, motionless for a moment.*)

*Everyone in the upstage row becomes lively, faces front. Someone comes
down and helps Helmert to his seat there. A party begins, where each in
turn entertains. Peter will smile and try to applaud every act. Gerard goes
around chatting with various audience members saying, "We're going to
put it on ourselves," etc. Then—*

ALL TOGETHER (*sing, two or three times through*)
    Come on in, take your hat off,
    Come on in, and just pull up a chair,
    Settle down, and make yourself at home,
    All your worries, leave them out there.

* GERARD (*with an accordion, sits on a chair on the small platform, just in
   front of the group*)
    Quiet everybody. Quiet. (*Laughs.*) I'll explain it to you. That
is not to say that I need to make an announcement, but here
it is: For you and for all of us I have especially composed
a piece that I call "The Crossing." Ladies and gentlemen,
"The Crossing."

*Gerard plays his accordion, a simple melody in two parts: the first, lilting;
the second, somber. Applause from the others.*

(*Laughs.*) "The Crossing." Yeah. "The Crossing." (*Returns to the
upstage row.*)

* RENSE (*standing on the small platform, one hand in his vest pocket*)
    Perhaps there are some among you . . .

Calls of "quiet," "ssst." Laughter.

Perhaps there are some among you who know the painting
by Brueghel entitled "The Fall of Icarus."

Whispers of "Huh?" and nodding.

In that painting you see Icarus, who with his waxen wings
has come too close to the sun and is beginning to fall. In a
few seconds he'll be dead. But in the same painting you see a

Actors'
Comments
———

Joop: I put Rense down. He's easy prey. Then I announce that I'm going to do a coin trick, but I get too angry, I get too tense, too red in the face, and it goes wrong. When I build up slowly, the scene works sometimes. It's a bit of a "laugh-ending" or "applause-ending." Dangerously close to "doing a number." Difficult!

farmer, and the farmer continues to plow, for life goes on: planting and harvesting, and sweat, so that in the autumn you can eat the fruit. The fruit of . . . the sweet fruit of pain. It is still summer; soon it will be winter. And in that same painting . . . And in that same painting you see a breeze coming over the water and even filling a sail of a ship at the shore, as if Brueghel wanted to call to Icarus:
(*Sings.*)
> Listen, listen friend beguiled,
> In all our hearts there plays a child
> Alone, and yet so bold
> He'd catch the ball of gold.
> Listen, my child,
> The wind is blowing wild

. . . .

*JOOP (*rising, interrupting*)
So, now that was nothing. Go sit down. Well, are you going to do some more, or not?

Rense returns to the upstage row. Joop moves to the table down right, a glass in his hands.

Now that it's gotten quiet, I'll tell you what I'm going to do. I'm going to do a vanishing trick. (*Pulls a handkerchief and a coin out of his pocket.*) This is a glass, this is a handkerchief, and this is a penny. Now I'm going to make the penny disappear. I could have used a quarter or a guilder, just as well. That doesn't matter. But I have expressly chosen a penny. Not because it's smaller, for if you take a dime, you have a smaller thing than a penny. But I'll take a penny because I know that here behind me are sitting people who would never do it with a penny. Never. Because they think they are worth more, because they think they're really something. Nonsense. They'd only want to do it with a gold coin. I'm not like that. (*With rising ferocity.*) I'll take a penny because I will be myself, because I'm not ashamed of anything. I know that I'm worth more than a penny, and that's why I'll take a penny, because I know myself . . . and a gold coin I don't need. Not at all. I'll do it with a penny or not at all, and if it has to be, then I won't do it at all. (*Returns to the upstage row.*)

Peter begins to applaud. Others are perplexed. Yolande, with a guitar, sits on the small platform.

Yolande: In the party scene I try to enjoy something, whatever there is to enjoy. I feel quite ill but I become more lively.

Peter: I'm thinking, what terrific legs. I try to make contact with the little lady who is sitting beside me [Daria]. I put my hand on her knee.

Daria: I fix myself up a bit, look at the others, am pleased and a bit excited. I peer at the audience and look around happily with little eyes. I think it's all terribly amusing, and I have my purse on my lap. I follow attentively everything that happens and hope that it all stays so cozy. It should always be like that. I don't understand everything so well. For example, I think Rense extremely fascinating but strange. Nevertheless, I wonder whether he feels well. Van Beusekom makes me very uncomfortable, and I am relieved that it ends well. (You keep playing all of this, but I myself am always so fascinated by what each one does that it happens naturally. In fact, I am just watching.)

Herman: I invented this story, but some of the elements in it are very personal—the being Belgian [Herman is a Flemish-speaking Belgian]. The sort of jokes that are made about Belgians here in Holland—the kind the British make about Australians. And it lets me use associations I have with my father and my grand-

*YOLANDE (*sweetly*)

You don't know me. I know you quite well. I know people. I've lived in ten countries; I speak fifteen languages. But I don't boast about it. Just the opposite. I think it's quite common. Believe me, it's nothing at all. It means nothing. It seems sensational, but all that remains is the memory of the people. And when I think of them, then I remember my good friend, a marvelous person whom I knew when I lived in France—and I wouldn't talk to you about her if she had not been a very famous person, a person certainly known to the older people among you: Yvette Claudette! Tonight I would like to make her live again for you. Let's listen to Yvette Claudette, a love song by the great chanteuse.

Yolande sits, sings a chanson, and accompanies herself on the guitar. Now and then she interjects, speaking, the translation of a banal phrase. At the refrain she sticks her feet straight out in front of her, punctuating the rhythm by pointing her toes upward.

The chanson begins:

YOLANDE (*sings*)

Love is always changing weather,
Sun and rain, then both together.
On ne sait jamais très bien
Ce que le temps fera demain
Plaisir d'amour. (*Speaks.*) Joy of love.
(*Sings.*)
Look at my legs, my love, don't leave,
Et si tu me trouves attractive
Alors viens, viens, viens.
We'll start first with a little kiss,
Now I won't tell you where,
But it's all too well you know the place,
Mon chéri,
Donc viens, viens, viens.

(*Rises, bows, speaks.*) Yvette Claudette, ladies and gentlemen.
(*Returns to the upstage row.*)

* HERMAN (*coming downstage front*)

How do you drive a Belgian crazy? Huh? (*To a member of the audience.*) Do you know that one? How do you drive a Belgian bonkers? You put him in a round room and tell him, "The french fries are over in the corner." That kind of joke, I hate.

father. Like my fath.r, I always keep myself busy, working and doing things. My father's been retired for a month now. For thirty-five years he worked in the same factory; he really built it up. But in his last three years there, it was changing, automating, and he lost his importance. They let him sit in his office, but he didn't count anymore. His aggressive bitterness about that is something I can relate to.

Also, I saw my grandfather dying in almost the same circumstances as my father. He died in forty-four, on the day of the liberation of Belgium. He was pensioned, but he didn't have enough money to live on, even simply, so he was working for a grocer, pushing a handcart—leaving the house every morning at five.

Actors'
Comments
_____

That's the only memory I have of my grandfather: him, pushing the cart. He was very ill—had ulcers all his life—but every day he went out and worked, because although he was very thin, he was strong. When I'm playing, I'm aware of my body, which is tense most of the time—the same as my father and my grandfather. In this scene I'm aggressive only partly because I resent intellectual people looking down on working people. The real reason is something else. It's more that you work for your whole life—killing yourself, in fact—and it's not noted, it's not important.

Daria: I get up with my purse, which I put down on a chair. I stand and wait until everything is quiet. I imagine that the radio starts to play, and then I sing high and mechanically: "Schenkt man sich Rosen in Tirol," etc. Then suddenly I reach my limit, and I pour out all of my emotions—anger, grief, bitterness, longing, love. Expressionistic opera. At the end I decide to really scare them all with a joke: I act as if I'm going to stab myself to death with a breadknife. (When we were making the first version of *Twi-*

'Cause it just so happens that I'm Belgian, and my whole life
I've sold french fries and my wife and I pinched and squeezed,
and for that, for that we saved every penny. I always worked
for other bosses, but finally, after years and years of saving,
we put enough aside, and I got my own stand—here in Holland—because Belgian fries are so tasty. And was proud of
my stand, and my wife and I made it ourselves. I've always
been good with my hands, and we built and painted it. In
really beautiful colors. And I'll never forget, on the day of
the opening I got from the mayor, from the mayor yet, a bouquet, a bouquet. And I put it on top of my stand. (*Mimes taking
a picture from his vest pocket. Looks at it.*) I still have a photo of it
with me: February 4, 1954. (*Shows it to the audience.*) My wife is
also in it. (*Pause. Puts it away. Takes out a second picture.*) And this is
the photo from February 5, 1954—two hours after the fire.
      A blessing from God, my mother's gift
            had I for potatoes.
      While cooking, I laughed
            —my honesty everyone knows.
      But then Lady Luck handed me the bill,
            on a terrible day that she chose.
      The oil caught fire and no insurance—
      You all should learn from my sad experience.
      My sorrow now always mounts,
      And I say, in your life one thing counts:
      For the years' endurance
      Buy good insurance.

*Herman returns to the upstage row. Others: "Let's see the photos, pass
them around," etc.*

*Daria rises, puts her red handbag beside her on the small platform, and
begins to sing, demurely, tremulously—"Schenkt man sich Rosen in Tirol"
from the operetta* Der Vogelhändler, *by Zeller. She pitches it much too high.*

* DARIA
      Schenkt man sich Rosen in Tirol,
      Weiss man, was das bedeuten soll.
      Doch geb ich die Rosen nicht allein,
      Wir sind am Rhein—nahaaaa—ooooo

*She breaks into a vigorous mock Italian aria. And suddenly she begins to
scream something like this.*

light, Joop suggested an improvisation in which I am an opera singer who is killing herself, and I had to try to do that on the spot.) When they go for it, I feel the greatest pleasure; I'll enjoy the moment for a long time to come. I say very softly that it was only a joke. For me personally this is also a kind of release. I'm happy that I can laugh heartily and have some fun, that I've also found a way to show this side of me.

Peter: While Daria sings, I watch and think how beautiful she is, how wonderful her singing is. When she screams, I'm startled but I keep thinking that it's part of what she's doing, so I applaud approvingly. But when she pulls the knife out of her purse, I stop her, take the knife, and then—as if it were part of the act, and to deal with my own panic—I sing, "And we'll never let each other go."

Actors' Comments

Peter: For my part in the entertainment, I want to tell people about the kinds of pains I have, but I do it by showing how many kinds of medicine I have. I got that idea after one of our Evening Workshops [early previews with invited audiences] when a member of the audience told me about a woman in an old people's home who went around showing her pills and talking about her health problems to anyone who'd listen.

Io sono furioso
Tremulo molto
Deshonorata
Perchè? Perchè?
Io sono solo tutta triste
Lacrimas moltas
Presto Presto
Pericula rossa
Santa Lucia perdonne me

With enormous gestures and violent Italian lines, Daria points to her handbag, pulls a dagger out of it, and spreads her arms wide, ready to plunge the dagger into her breast.

Everyone leaps up, grabbing her arms. Someone secures the dagger. Chaos. And then in the middle of the confusion, one sees the little woman bent over, clutching her handbag, looking out at the audience—and laughing at her joke. All return to their seats, except—

* PETER (*sings a little, wants others to join in*)
And we'll never let each other go.
And we'll never let each other go.
And we'll never let each other go. (*Etc.*)

(*Steps forward. Mimes taking a little container of pills out of his right pocket, holds it up, explains, puts it into his left pocket; then takes out the next container, etc.*)

Quiet. I have them right here. Now look at this. (*Pointing behind him.*) They have all of these pills back there.

That is for when you fall asleep in the daytime instead of at night. If you take these, then you'll stay awake during the day and then you'll sleep at night. Therefore.

These. I have a whole bunch of these little pills. You see? That is: sometimes I don't have enough spit. To eat bread. Then it sticks so long in your mouth. And then if you want to say something, that's a nuisance.

These, I got from van Geffen. Little round things with a crack. I take one now and then, ah, Sundays. So with tea, if I don't have any visitors.

And these, that is in case I stop. Then I stay standing too long, on a path, eh? Maybe I stand, and then I take one of these, and I'll tell you, that's a pick-up. Yeah.

These . . . I stole them.

Helmert: We had a morning when people came to watch us, a group of youngsters, and we were to give each other directives for improvisations. Marja asked me to make up a song like a singing commercial on the radio. Well, I didn't like that. People have come to look at you and you have to do *that* in three minutes? It made me angry. So I put my anger into that song, and I made it up in three minutes, just like it is now. The problem for me is doing it like the old farm man. I know I talk the same as the man in my first two scenes [with Rense and Herman], but I don't feel like him. I'm not thinking in the first scene, "I'm a man who has lost a little son in an accident and makes a song about it." In my feeling the scenes aren't connected.

Joop: When we join in the singing, hesitantly at first, then all of us screeching, I get cold chills up my spine. That's good, awfully good.

Marja: I'm always inspired by Helmert when he laughs during that song. That gets to me every time.

These. I've forgotten now what these were for, but I take one every once in a while.

(*Takes another container, examines it, shakes his head, silently puts it away. Then the next—*)

And these I have sometimes if I start to sort of cry a little. My eyes fill with tears. That's not sadness. That's my glands. Then I have one of these. Yeah. Those are fun. And . . . More, I don't have. I'm not a braggart, or anything. (*Turns toward upstage row, pause.*) Maybe some of you have pills left over. . . . (*Sits.*)

Helmert rises hesitantly, comes forward, holding a pair of glasses and a sheet of paper.

JOOP
Now we can go home. We can leave. Time to go home.

*HELMERT
People will think it's strange that I also step forward to do something. I'm not a leader. Everybody knows that. I sit in the lounge and usually stare silently out the window. But I wanted to tell you, that's not without reason. I have a reason. In life we all have our share of sorrow, and about my share of sorrow I myself have made the following song. And I want to sing it for you—(*Puts on glasses and sings from his paper.*)
    The traffic rushed on by,
    The autos took a child—
    They tried to brake, but on the roadway he had
                    landed,
    And there his parents stood beside so empty handed.
    If the people at the wheel could only feel it—
    How from their murd'rous speeding
    Many parents' hearts are bleeding.
    A crash can happen now and then,
    But your child you can never have again.

**Others begin to join in, hesitantly.*

    If the people at the wheel could only feel it—
    . . . .

Finally, everyone sings loudly, locking arms and rocking back and forth. Helmert is surprised, confused, pleased, and, in the end, sings it out.

    If the people at the wheel could only feel it—
    . . . .

Marja: Yolande and I created this scene in two minutes. Never rehearsed it. It plays itself. We created it so quickly because we knew what we meant immediately in connection with Bergman's film *Cries and Whispers*; we both had a special fondness for that film. Of course, I've known Yolande for about twenty years. We were in the same school as children, and both of us have had the experience of having a child.

It's rather the same thing, I think—having a child and dying. You feel it that way, a bit. You have to give in. When you have a pain and you resist, the pain gets worse. What you do is, you don't resist the pain. But when I had a child, I couldn't do it. I thought, if I don't resist the pain, I will die. When you're playing, it's the same way. You have to give in.

On stage, I just happen to appear when Yolande is about to die, and I see right away that she has to give in, that's all. If you comfort somebody, it's easier for them to give in. When you're on the edge of crying and somebody's nice to you, you cry, and then you get rid of it. When I'm doing this scene, I feel how easy it could be to die, what a little thing it is. I'm glad I'm with Yolande to have that experience with her, so that when I die I'll feel the same way too, like a leaf that falls from a branch. That's what I experience. I never feel sentimental, even though I cry every time. I don't know how that happens.

Helmert returns to the upstage row.

Yolande slowly comes forward and sits quietly stage center, facing the audience, her hands folded in her lap. Silence.

* MARJA (*entering from off right, sees Yolande, stops at the edge of the playing area*)

Can't you sleep? Does it hurt somewhere, love?

Yolande shakes her head "no."

Love (*coming over to Yolande*), what a pretty face you have. A sweet body. (*Standing behind Yolande, arranging her hair.*) Shall I do your hair for you? So. Very gently. (*Both look straight ahead as if into a mirror.*) See how pretty you are? Beautiful. You haven't changed at all. See?

YOLANDE (*left hand drops, relaxed, by her side*)

Yes.

MARJA

Hey, shall I come and sit with you? (*Pulling a chair over to Yolande's left.*) I'll just get a chair. I'm not going away. I'm just getting a chair. (*Sits.*) Hold on to me, hold on to me. Love, you're as yellow as a canary.

Yolande gives a half sigh, half cough.

Shall I just go and get a wet washcloth? No? Hold on to me.

YOLANDE (*coughs, doubles over onto Marja's lap*)

I can't hold it back. Nobody. Don't get anybody. Don't get anybody.

MARJA

No. Doesn't matter. Let it go. Let it go. No. Let it go. Doesn't matter at all.

YOLANDE (*stands*)

I don't want to . . .

MARJA (*with her arm around Yolande*)

No. I'll hold you, tight.

YOLANDE

I don't want to . . .

MARJA

Sure.

YOLANDE

I don't want to. (*Sinks back into the chair. Coughs into Marja's lap.*)

Yolande: It was Marja's idea to show something where one person [Marja] accepts everything [vomit, helplessness] from the other [Yolande] and through this genuinely "helps" the other to be complete and thus able to die. There's an analogy here with giving birth, another situation where complete concentration is needed. In this scene I'm not so much afraid of dying as afraid of letting go, of losing control; I'm concentrating all my energies on holding myself together. Also, I don't want to be a burden to anyone—I'm a bit like an animal that withdraws from others when it's dying.

When Marja appears, that's a shock. It affects me in a powerful emotional way, because now I don't have to die alone. She makes me relax, sometimes by laughing—which means wetting my pants. Still, I feel shame and fear, fear that someone will be called. But Marja helps me accept that. Then, after I throw up, there is relaxation, but I still feel powerless, ashamed. When I say, "Your nice robe, I can't clean it," and so on, all of that starts the dying part. I want the audience to experience an analogy with orgasm and birth but not very consciously. With me, too, this analogy must remain vague and not take on too much meaning. Marja really leads this whole scene—I just *accompany* her. When this works it's a fine experience, because I don't have to do anything; everything just happens to me. In general throughout this scene I certainly want to make things clear for myself but often not too conscious. I prepare myself for the scene by trying to concentrate on being wholly open and blank toward everything that happens. That often gives me a chance to slip in somewhere.

MARJA

Let yourself go, now. Let it go. Love.

YOLANDE

Oh, God. Your nice robe.

MARJA

No. That doesn't matter. Doesn't matter.

Yolande cries out.

No, no, precious. That doesn't bother me at all. I can clean it up easy. No, no, precious. That doesn't . . . I won't get anybody. (*Caressing Yolande's face, Yolande resting her head on Marja's shoulder.*) No, no, precious. It doesn't bother me at all. I'll clean it up. No, no. It doesn't bother me at all. There. There. (*Kissing Yolande's face.*) Don't you see? No. It doesn't bother me at all, love. Let it go, my precious.

YOLANDE (*crying, coughing*)

I can't. I can't.

MARJA

Sure. Let it go. Let it go. Let it go. Sure. There. Sò.

YOLANDE

It's coming, it's coming. Please, no. Please, no. (*Lurches over onto Marja's lap, motionless.*)

MARJA

It's fine. It's fine. It's fine.

Yolande sighs. Silence.

Ah. A little sigh, a little sigh (*raising up Yolande's head to rest on her right shoulder, kissing Yolande's face*), a little sigh, a little sigh. O, love, I'm so . . . (*tears running down Marja's face*) . . . so happy about it, so happy . . . It's OK. You don't have to be afraid of anything. I know it. I know it. It is a little sigh. It's OK, love.

I'll go and wash you. Take off your clothes, wash you, a clean towel, soap.

Come on, love. I won't get anybody else.

Come on, love.

Herman: Like Marja, I'm pretty quick with my tongue, and I like to make jokes, so I find what she does here very, very good. In the last scene you really see the other side of that woman.

Gerard: I think we could change the last scene, so that Yolande is not always the one who is dying, but everybody gets a turn. Then each of us could reinterpret all our scenes in the light of that last one, when we have to die. That could be a new dimension.

Shireen Strooker (the stimulator): I think that ideally everyone should do this scene sometime, but only when I think the time is right for that.

Peter: During this scene I experience being present at the end, the farewell, and I feel like I'm on a rickety bridge. I can't move anymore. My neck gets hard and stiff, but inside I'm melting: little by little everything is becoming fluid.

Joop: Sitting, listening to the scene between Marja and Yolande—God, how beautiful.

With Yolande's head on her right shoulder, Marja stands, lifting Yolande with her. Marja puts Yolande's arms over her shoulders, grasps her around the waist almost as if to dance with her, and slowly begins pulling her toward stage left. Yolande seems a great doll, feet slightly dragging. Marja is moving backward, tears streaming down her face.

So . . . Come on. Easy, easy. We have lots of time. Put your arm around me. And the other one. So. There we go. Come on, love. Come on . . . love. (*Marja pulls Yolande all the way across the stage and up left, as—*)

Music comes up—a Dixieland blues number.

Notes on the Text

Music

The following familiar Dutch songs were used in the performance:

"Look for Sun Beams" ("Zoek de zon op")

"Although My Tire's a Little Flat" ("Al is mijn achterband wat zacht"; a variation on the line "Mijn achterband is wel wat zacht," from the song "Spring maar achterop")*

"Tonia, Tonia"

"When the Bell of Arnemuiden" ("Als de klok van Arnemuiden")

"And the Two of Us, We're Better as a Pair" ("Met z'n tweeën is het beter dan alleen")

"Look in My Eyes and See the Tiny People" ("Kijk eens naar de poppetjes in mijn ogen"; published as "Kijk eens in de poppetjes van m'n ogen")*

"Oh, How Pretty You Are" ("O, wat ben je mooi")

"Come on in, Take Your Hat Off" ("Kom d'r in, zet je hoed af")

Peter Faber made up the refrain "And we'll never let each other go" ("En we laten mekaar niet los").

The four lines as Daria sings them from the operetta *Der Vogelhändler*, by Carl Zeller, read in English:

* Sheet music from the Netherlands Theater Institute, Amsterdam.

When you give rosés in the Tyrol,
Everyone knows what that means.
But I'm not giving you roses alone,
We're on the Rhine . . .

In the libretto (Leipzig: Bosworth, 1891) the last two lines read, "Doch trifft der Brauch bei uns nicht ein, / Wir sind am Rhein, bedenk', am Rhein!" (But we don't have the custom here, / We're on the Rhine, just think, the Rhine!).

Textual Variants

Soon after this tape was made, the Werkteater eliminated the following scene from subsequent performances of *Twilight*. When it was included in some of the early productions, it just preceded the party scene.

Each actor stands and speaks as if making an announcement.

YOLANDE

When a person has died, they lay him in a coffin lined with silk, either in pyjamas or in a shirt. If his neck is somewhat sunken in, a tie is really good too. And, you can say farewell to the deceased in the funeral parlor. In the background is the sound of pleasant—sorry—quiet music. Don't forget to bring a picture, so before the coffin is closed they can see that it's really him.

JOOP

The flowers. The flowers may be placed on or against the coffin, depending on the quantity. Most common—usually presented by family, or personnel, or management—is a wreath, while a single branch has something especially personal about it. Also a single arum-lily or a small bunch of violets, purple in color, if placed modestly—that is, not in the center—can also express genuine humility.

DARIA

The furnace. The furnace is heated to a temperature of 400 or 500 degrees centigrade, which causes the coffin to catch fire by itself. Then there is the skimmer, which removes the hard parts, like zippers and pushbuttons, handles, bolts and nuts, after which the whole thing drops through a strainer.

Then there is the centrifuge, through which the real, hot, pure bone ashes remain.

These are presented in a kind of drum, and then they may be poured out either over the North Sea, or over the Rhine, or here over the terrain where there is such a wealth of flowers.

In the party scene, instead of the "fries in the corner" riddle, Herman tells a joke that is difficult to translate: "Three naked men are standing in a row. One of the three is Belgian. How can you tell? Do you know that joke? By his *puntzakje.*" *Puntzakje* means "pointed sack," a paper cone from which Belgians commonly eat french fries. Belgians are supposedly addicted to french fries. *Zakje* means "little sack" and also "scrotum."

Sources for the Actors' Comments

The actors' comments on the pages facing the text of *Twilight*, and throughout the book, were collected during the spring of 1975 from the following tape-recorded interviews with the actors and from their written notes to the author. The actors have reviewed and approved the statements as published.

Joop Admiraal to Dunbar Ogden and Rob Erenstein, 11 February 1975. Written notes in Dutch.

Joop Admiraal with Ogden, 8 March 1975, Amsterdam. Taped interview in English, transcribed by Gillian Bagwell.

Yolande Bertsch to Ogden and Erenstein, 11 February 1975. Written notes in Dutch.

Yolande Bertsch with Ogden, 25 May 1975, Bussum (near Amsterdam). Taped interview in English, transcribed by Gillian Bagwell.

Cas Enklaar with Ogden, 11 June 1975, Amsterdam. Taped interview in English, transcribed by Susan Lam.

Peter Faber to Ogden and Erenstein, 11 February 1975. Written notes in Dutch.

Peter Faber with Ogden, 22 February 1975, Soest (near Amsterdam). Taped interview in English, transcribed by Gillian Bagwell.

Frank Groothof with Ogden, 26 June 1975, Amsterdam. Taped interview in English, transcribed by Cristopher Berns.

Marja Kok with Ogden, 25 February 1975, Amsterdam. Taped interview in English, transcribed by Gillian Bagwell.

Marja Kok to Ogden and Erenstein, 21 May 1975. Written notes in Dutch.

Marja Kok with Ogden, 11 June 1975, Amsterdam. Taped interview in English, transcribed by Gillian Bagwell.

Hans Man in't Veld with Ogden, 29 May 1975, Amsterdam. Taped interview in English, transcribed by Cristopher Berns.

Hans Man in't Veld with Ogden, 6 June 1975, Amsterdam. Taped interview in English, transcribed by Cristopher Berns.

Daria Mohr to Ogden and Erenstein, 2 February 1975. Written notes in Dutch.

Daria Mohr with Ogden, 4 June 1975. Taped interview in English, transcribed by Gillian Bagwell.

Rense Royaards to Ogden and Erenstein, 11 February 1975. Written notes in Dutch.

Rense Royaards with Ogden, 26 May 1975, Amsterdam. Taped interview in English, transcribed by Susan Lam.

Shireen Strooker with Ogden, 22 February 1975, Soest (near Amsterdam). Taped interview in English, transcribed by Gillian Bagwell.

Gerard Thoolen with Ogden, 24 May 1975, Amsterdam. Taped interview in English, transcribed by Cristopher Berns.

Herman Vinck with Ogden, 13 April 1975, Amsterdam. Taped interview in English, transcribed by Gillian Bagwell.

Helmert Woudenberg with Ogden, 27 February 1975, Amsterdam. Taped interview in English, transcribed by Cristopher Berns.

Helmert Woudenberg with Ogden, 6 June 1975, Amsterdam. Taped interview in English, transcribed by Gillian Bagwell.

Olga Zuiderhoek with Ogden, 2 June 1975, Amsterdam. Taped interview in English, transcribed by Cristopher Berns.

II

Essays on Performance Dynamics in the Werkteater

4

Playmaking

The Experience
of the Actors

The alternative theater movement today includes a rebirth of active and sustained collaboration between performers and writers of plays. Moreover, for an art theater as defined by Lång-backa—a theater that tries to express the values of the performing group, to reach a new audience, to build a clear repertory in which individual productions support each other, and to search for new working methods—the desire to create plays of its own is wholly logical. The Moscow Art Theater and the Berliner Ensemble, to name two of the theaters studied by Långbacka, had Chekhov and Brecht, respectively, as resident playwrights. The actors of the Werkteater went further. Instead of searching for a playwright, they made playmaking itself an intimate part of their new working methods.

As we have seen in the log of *Twilight,* the company took this radical decision as a means of developing themselves as actors. It was not their conscious intention to fill a need for strong, contemporary playwriting in the Netherlands, and yet I believe that is just what they did. In this sense theirs is a happy accident: with their productions they show today's playwrights the vitality and the depth that can come from close collaboration with actors. In fact, the Werkteater troupe demonstrates by example that all writers of plays should have experience as actors.

The log of *Twilight* has already shown us many of the methods the Werkteater has used in its playmaking process. Here we shall look closely at a single scene from that production in an effort to discover how the process springs from the inner person of the actor, how it evolves through the on-stage relationship between two actors, and how it can create a powerful personal communication between actor and audience.

Rense Royaards approaches the easy chair in which Helmert Woudenberg sits and rolls it (it is on casters) to the front of the playing area. Rense stands behind and slightly to one side of the chair and does not move until the scene is almost over. Helmert remains seated. As two men in a home for the elderly, exploring the sensations of becoming old, they reminisce about their childhoods. Rense begins.[1]

RENSE

> Let's go sit in the sunshine. So. Here's your spot. Look how the sun's shining. Every time spring comes I get that same high feeling I used to have when I went with my parents to that little village by the dunes. We got on the train in Amsterdam, and we sang all the way.
>
> (*Sings.*)
>
>> Look for sun beams,
>> They are so fine,
>> For a ray of sunshine
>> That must be mine.
>
> And then in Alkmaar we changed to a little steam train.

Here Rense is remembering visits to Schoorl and Bergen, the seashore area outside of Amsterdam, where he actually grew up as a city boy. Helmert, who was raised in very different circumstances, on a small farm in Hoofddorp, reacts to Rense through association with the train.

HELMERT (*now sitting stage center*)

> My father didn't like trains at all. He said they didn't exist. And so when we boys found a paper or a magazine with a picture of a train, we took it to him and said, "Dad, this is a

1. The text is from a live performance of *Twilight* tape-recorded at the Werkteater, Amsterdam, 15 November 1974, transcribed by Emmy Koobs and translated by Ogden. For the Dutch text of this scene, see Appendix C.

train!" Then he'd get fiery red, and he'd stand up, snatch the paper from the table, rush to the door, turn around and say, "Traitors!" Then he'd go to the outhouse and wipe his ass with it.

This dialogue was not written down and then memorized. The lines printed here were transcribed from a tape-recording of a performance. The actors had developed the scene and the text from improvisations on a situation they had chosen. During the improvisation process, which can take weeks and sometimes months, each actor creates a character out of himself: out of bits and pieces of his experience, out of stories he has heard, out of people he knows. Writers of plays work in this way, too. But in Rense and in Helmert, each figure exists in the present moment, so that each is shaped by immediate contact with the other and with the audience.

Rense now associates the sound of the word *reet* (*crack* or *arse*) with *reed* (*rode*, the past tense of *to ride*).

RENSE (*standing beside Helmert's chair*)
And then you rode. Under a radiant sky, you rode along the North Holland Canal. And then at the windmill of Koedijk you turned into the polder [field reclaimed from the sea]. And it was like a god's hand had strewn the pastures full of flowers. And the birds were in the air. And the ditches were full of duckweed and ducks.

Helmert's associations with the polder ditches create sharp contrasts that soon develop into grotesques.

HELMERT
The polder ditches were fifteen feet wide or more. And there were men from Brabant—hired hands—and they were work-ing for us. They would kick off their wooden shoes, take a run, and jump clear over that ditch! Fifteen feet or more! What men! God!
RENSE
And then you arrived at that little station under the trees. And Roland Holst stood there with his walking stick. And

then you got off the train and you smelled the sea air, mixed with the steam from the locomotive.

HELMERT

And there was a woman with the Brabant people—that was one tough woman. She could fight and work like the men. And if you gave her a quarter, with her bare hands she'd catch a rat from the threshing floor and bite its head off! Aagh, like a chunk of bread.

RENSE

And then we hiked through the dunes to the sea. And there was that day when we saw a rabbit, leaping and dodging. We ran, ran, ran after it, and I don't know how it happened, but then . . .

HELMERT

Saturday the children had their bath. They were all rounded up. Their clothes were taken off. And then, like puppies they were dumped into the tub. They sloshed, and they splashed, and they laughed. That was so much fun. . . .

RENSE

Then I tripped. I tripped.

HELMERT

The other day a little boy fell off the roof.

RENSE

And a trickle ran down my chin, and great red drops dripped on my white suit.

By this time a transformation has taken place. In the act of recalling, the two men have become the children they once were, and spectators in the theater feel a wonderful transparency about them: Helmert, still sitting in his chair, reaches out for Rense, eventually takes him on his knee, and begins to bounce him up and down.

HELMERT

O little boy, come here. Children should play. They mustn't be sick. Come over here, little friend, come here, my little boy. My little man. (*Takes Rense by the hand, then onto his knee.*) And when they're sick, then you keep them busy all day long. Then you play one game after the other, and you never get tired, because they have to get better, the little ones. So they can play again.

My little boy, O little boy, my little friend. You even smell sick. Your father isn't here. Your mother isn't here. But I'm with you. (*Tears run down Rense's cheeks.*) You'll get well. Then you can play again. One game after the other. (*Bounces Rense up and down, more vigorously at each line of the child's chant.*)

So goes the master's horse, and the master's horse
goes so.
And so goes the lady's horse, and the lady's horse
goes so.
And so goes the farmer's horse, and the farmer's horse
goes so!

Helmert slumps a little to one side. Rense stands up and begins to push the chair up left.

Toward the end of the scene Helmert chants louder and louder. Rense, sitting on Helmert's knee, stares vacantly ahead, and tears begin to run down his cheeks. Helmert the old man has become a young Helmert caring for a child, and old Rense has become Rense the injured child. Each has entered a very particular *state of mind*—a much more accurate expression than *dramatic character*.

The progress of this scene and the manner in which it evolved show us how the actors enter this state of mind and how they found it in rehearsal. First Rense and Helmert connect, in the emotions of remembering; and then, without moving and only in the speaking, they start to live in events of their childhood. In their first improvisations, Rense and Helmert had established themselves as two distinct individuals from very different backgrounds who could reminisce and interact associatively. But they remained rather separate. Then each learned how to slip into the very child he was remembering. And finally, after some months, they discovered that by creating on stage a relationship between an older person and a child, they could bring together in one theatrical moment the deeply personal past and the deeply personal present.

As illustrated by this scene, it was by going back to the origins of acting that the members of the Werkteater began to develop their playmaking techniques. Rense and Helmert created their own language because that language is part of their own experience. Language happens to be very important to them because they are very verbal people. They wanted to discover an experience of the past in the present, to make it clear for themselves, and then to make it clear for an audience. And so they began not with acting but with themselves—a process that is radically different from playing according to texts written by others.

"We choose a structure," says Rense, "where writing, inventing, and playing are one thing."[2] The words, sounds, rhythms, and images they create—and the connotations, interactions, and ambience of these—are all rooted in that native earth where language and experience remain inseparable. When they performed, the tensions of stage presentation and an onstage relationship heightened and focused their speech, so that audience members not only recognized their own voices but also felt familiar currents of electricity passing between the actors, currents that generate a force greater than the words themselves. Everyday language grew into a very special kind of mimetic poetry, a language that is larger than life.

In 1982 the critic John Peereboom said: "Up to now nearly all plays performed in Holland have been foreign or *poetic*," and the speech taught in the theater schools has been "rather petty, false, unnatural." "The Werkteater," he added, "has taught the Dutch to speak normal Dutch on stage and to speak it in a normal way."[3] Precisely because it was thoroughly Dutch and contemporary, the language of the Werkteater presented no intellectual, cultural, or historical barriers. Actor and audience could affirm each other spontaneously on the same emotional wavelength. The spectator could say: "Yes, there I am."

Without the resources of contemporary native playwriting

2. Rense Royaards, *Werkteater, teaterwerk sinds 1970* (Utrecht: Van Boekhoven-Bosch, 1980), 144.

3. From interview in English, John Peereboom with Ogden, 14 May 1982, Amsterdam.

for training and performance, how can a normal actor portray a person in his own living room, in present time, with the authenticity that comes from experiencing a personal truth? How can an actor touch his innermost being if during his training and his career he has rarely had the opportunity to make sustained explorations of language, character, and situation that are intimate to himself? By the same token, how can a theatergoer react other than distantly or intellectually when he never sees acting and playwriting in the theater that bring him face to face with himself (as opposed to film and television, which stay close to native ground)? But if a spectator does experience spontaneous self-recognition, as at the Werkteater, then he or she can go on to find greater personal truth in performances of Sophocles, Shakespeare, and Strindberg.

As Frank Rich put it recently in the *New York Times*, in the United States today there is a "widespread impression that American plays simply do not matter anymore." "The best plays," he also wrote, "arise not from the agenda of journalism or politics, but from the private agenda of the writer's sensibility."[4] Unfortunately, the American theatrical writer usually lives at some distance from the performer, physically as well as psychologically. In certain areas of the alternative theater movement, that condition is changing; but with a handful of exceptions, our dramatists still tend to work in isolation, separated during the initial creative process from the mysterious pulse of stage timing and deprived of daily contact, except perhaps as a spectator, with the sound, sight, smell, touch, and taste of performing.

If we look closely at the dramatists whose work has lived through the ages, we discover that nearly all of them had long periods of intimacy with the living material of the theatrical event. Molière as actor-playwright is a vivid example. As Roger Herzel writes, it is "likely that each character, at every stage of his development in Molière's mind, must have been directly tied to the imagined performance on stage of the actor to whom he was to be assigned: speaking with that actor's voice, gesturing

---

4. Frank Rich, "To Make Serious Theater, 'Serious' Issues Aren't Enough," *New York Times*, 19 February 1984, H2, H24.

with his gestures, moving with his awkwardness or grace, lightness or heaviness, timing his replies and reactions to the other imaginary actors on the imaginary stage just as Molière had seen him do countless times on the real stage."[5] It is this sort of intimacy that informs the playwriting process of the Werkteater actors.

5. Roger Herzel, *The Original Casting of Molière's Plays* (Ann Arbor, Mich.: UMI Research Press, 1981), 1. Herzel gives an indication of this relationship between creators and creation in his note on Molière's writing for Mlle. de Brie after Molière's new young wife had replaced Mlle. de Brie as the first lady of the company (p. 87): "some of the most ambiguous, disquieting, and, in a word, interesting characters, male or female, in Molière's work are those which were written for Mlle. de Brie—Arsinoé, Alcmène, Dorimène, Armande, Béline—after she had technically ceased to be the troupe's leading actress."

5

Metamorphosis

The Actors
and the Audience

During a theatrical production audience members tend to "imitate" the performers in front of them. It is not that they "pretend" to be like the actors, or consciously "mimic" them. Rather, they begin, for the most part unconsciously, to feel a little like the actor or actress on the stage. An inner metamorphosis occurs.

This sort of metamorphosis, of course, is central to the theories of Artaud, who said that through breathing as well as other physical connections, the identification between the actor's body and the spectator's body is established. "This is the chain that links them together," Martin Esslin has written; it is what, in Artaud's words, "allows the spectator to identify himself with the performance breath by breath, and bar by bar. . . . All emotion has organic bases." Artaud imagined that audiences might actually begin to breathe in rhythm with an actor—and we now know that this can indeed occur.[1]

This same kind of imitation has been described by the *New York Times* critic John Martin, the first person to attempt an aesthetic of modern dance. In *The Modern Dance* (1933), he wrote: "Through kinesthetic sympathy you respond to the impulse of the dancer." Later, in "Dance as a Means of Communication" (1946), he spelled out his hypothesis more specifically: "Because

1. Martin Esslin, *Antonin Artaud* (London: John Calder, 1976), 87.
   Antonin Artaud, *The Theater and Its Double*, trans. Mary C. Richards (New York: Grove Press, 1958), 141.

of the inherent contagion of bodily movement, which makes the onlooker feel sympathetically in his own musculature the exertions he sees in somebody else's musculature, the dancer is able to convey through movement the most intangible emotional experience. This is the prime purpose of the modern dance." In fact, certain studies in the field of semiotics have now moved further in the directions suggested earlier by Artaud and Martin.[2]

Many people who attended productions of the Werkteater experienced this transformation. It is emotional as well as physical, and because of the actors' special qualities, it has at its heart a deep sense of play. An examination of the final scene of *Twilight*, illustrated by photographs, will reveal some of the roots of this metamorphosis.[3] Here Marja Kok and Yolande Bertsch are residents of an old people's home. During these moments Yolande (dressed in black) is dying and Marja is taking care of her. The photographs emphasize the power in the facial expressions of the actresses and the closeness of the actresses to their audiences—two major elements in the experience of metamorphosis.

2. John Martin, *The Modern Dance* (New York: A. S. Barnes, 1933), 12; *The Dance* (New York: Tudor, 1946), 105.

Jack Anderson, "Pioneer of Dance Criticism," *New York Times*, 12 June 1983, H10.

In 1968, Nelson Goodman asserted that "what we know through art [in general] is felt in our bones and nerves and muscles as well as grasped by our minds." *Languages of Art* (Indianapolis: Bobbs-Merrill, 1968), 259.

Eleanor Metheny, like Martin, goes on to point to the transformations within the spectator as the chief means of communication, noting that the onlooker senses his or her own experiences as triggered by the performer: "the kinesthetic perceptions which we may identify with our recognition of a movement form performed by another person are not perceptions of *his* sensations. Rather, we experience these sensations within ourselves. Such sensations can only be elicited by the pressures, pulls, and tensions of our own muscle contractions or by the effect of our own movements." *Movement and Meaning* (New York: McGraw-Hill, 1968), 37–38.

In his book *The Dance*, Joost Merloo goes even further: "Coughing, laughter, crying, yawning, itching, scratching, shivering, rocking—all these produce the same inadvertent reactions in fellow beings." He says that these "so-called archaic body-movements and body signs are empathy-provoking." And then he reaches back to the realm of prenatal experience in order to formulate his psychological rule for imitative behavior in performer-audience communication: "*the more a human expression reminds us of our own infantile (and intrauterine) world, the more contagious is this expression* [Merloo's italics]." (Philadelphia: Chilton, 1960), 36.

3. The photographs were taken during performance by Bruce Gray. This scene became the starting point for the Werkteater film *In for Treatment*, which won the Prix d'Italia for television drama in 1980 and became the official Dutch entry for Best Foreign Language Film at the Academy Awards in the following year. This scene from *Twilight* foreshadows especially the end of *In for Treatment*, where two men, cancer patients, lie side by side in hospital beds.

FIGURE 6. Marja: "Can't you sleep?"

FIGURE 7.
Marja: "Love, what
a pretty face you have."

FIGURE 8.
Marja: "Shall I do
your hair for you?"

FIGURE 9. Yolande
(*left hand drops, relaxed,
by her side*): "Yes."

FIGURE 10.
Marja: "I'm
not going away."

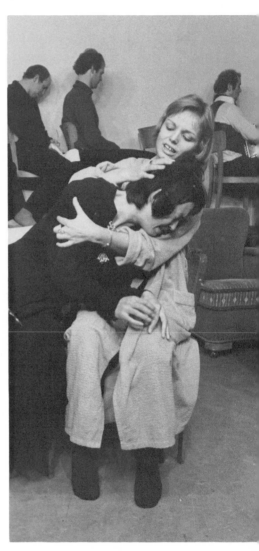

FIGURE 11.
Marja:
"Hold on to me."

FIGURE 12. Yolande: "I can't
hold it back. Nobody.
Don't get anybody."

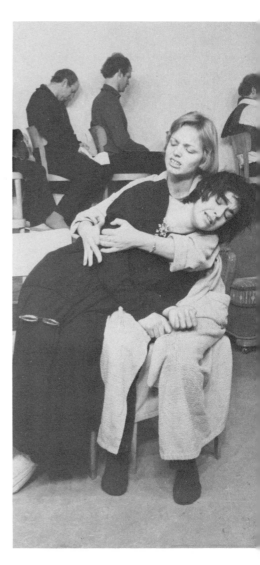

FIGURE 13.
Marja: "Let it go.
Let it go."

FIGURE 14.
Yolande:
"I don't want to . . ."

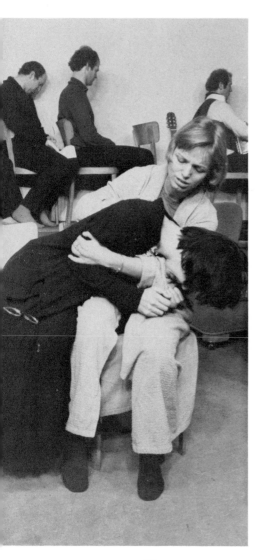

FIGURE 15.
Yolande (*coughs
into Marja's lap*): "Oh, God.
Your nice robe."

FIGURE 16. Marja:
"No, no, precious.
That doesn't bother
me at all."

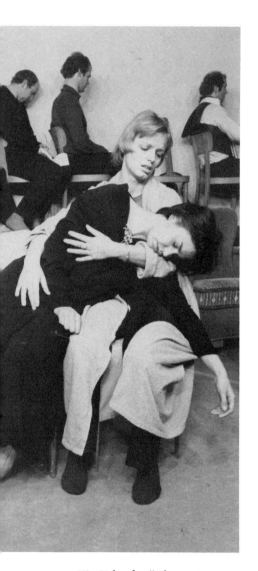

FIGURE 17. Yolande: "It's coming, it's coming. Please, no. Please, no." (*Lurches over onto Marja's lap, motionless.*)

FIGURE 18.
Marja:
"A little sigh,
a little sigh."

FIGURE 19.
Marja: "It's OK, love.
I'll go and wash you."

FIGURES 20 and 21. Marja
(*grasps Yolande's body around
the waist almost as if to dance
with her, and slowly begins
pulling her toward stage left.*)

The underlying dynamic of this scene is a playing with death, which reminds one of the medieval theater. Here the embracing of Marja and Yolande includes the acceptance of vomit and urine as part of all that is human, as Yolande lets herself go into dying. It is this attitude on the part of the two women that those in the audience absorb, and it is in their dance of death that the audience participates. To some degree the spectators share the emotional struggle that is being played out before them, and when Yolande sighs and there is silence, they feel an inner peace.

What is the engine of this metamorphosis, and how does it compare with that sought by the Werkteater's spiritual forebears? In *The Constant Prince* Grotowski had his spectators gather around the protagonist, as if to spy on a secret act, whereas in *The Cenci* Artaud attacked his spectators with the cruelty of cries and groans. In the work of both men there is an overt drive toward therapy, a desire to improve the inner condition of the audience. The Werkteater never had such a motive, and tried to connect with its audiences in a very different way.

When Marja Kok and Yolande Bertsch started to develop their scene in *Twilight*, they had been working together in the Werkteater company for three years. At one point Yolande suggested to Marja that she think of herself as "a woman who is a bit mad, who is a bit feebleminded—a very instinctive woman, who . . . isn't rational." As Marja said, she then imagined herself a woman who pushes along a doll carriage and talks to the doll, saying whatever comes into her head. This free associating gave Marja an inner freedom and a certain naïveté, a special openness to the dynamics of performance throughout *Twilight*.

Some notes Yolande wrote on the making of this scene also illustrate the use of inner resources in this method of playwriting.

It was Marja's idea to show something where one person [Marja] accepts everything [vomit, helplessness] from the other [Yolande] and through this genuinely "helps" the other to be complete and thus able to die. There's an analogy here with giving birth, another situation where complete concentration is needed. In this scene I'm not so much afraid of dying as afraid of letting go, of losing control; I'm concentrating all my energies on holding myself together. Also, I don't want to be a burden to anyone—I'm a bit like an animal that withdraws from others when it's dying.[4]

Clearly, Yolande is not talking about a dramatic character as an external entity. She is talking about living an inner condition: her own fear of letting go and her own effort to concentrate her energies. Marja, as we have seen, found a contrasting inner condition for Yolande to play against—a certain naïveté and a liberation of spirit in free associating. In her notes, Yolande goes on to reveal the bond that had developed between them.

When Marja appears, that's a shock. It affects me in a powerful emotional way, because now I don't have to die alone. She makes me relax, sometimes by laughing—which means wetting my pants. Still, I feel shame and fear, fear that someone will be called. But Marja helps me accept that. Then, after I throw up, there is relaxation, but I still feel powerless, ashamed. When I say, "Your nice robe, I can't clean it," and so on, all of that starts the dying part. I want the audience to experience an analogy with orgasm and birth but not very consciously. With me, too, this analogy must remain vague and not take on too much meaning.

Marja also thinks searchingly about herself in relationship to the role she created. She says that in life, "I'd rather help than be helped," and that "essentially I don't want people to get too near me." When I asked whether personally it is easy for her to take care of someone who is sick or in pain, she said simply, "I don't know. I don't know."[5]

Right after *Twilight* had become a regular part of the repertory, Marja suggested to Yolande that the two of them try exchanging roles. But Yolande told her, "I'm not quite the character to comfort people, in the play." Nevertheless, during the first months of *Twilight*, Marja subtly altered her approach to her own role. "Now I try to be more responsive," she said. "When I play now with Yolande, I wait far more. I respond, as far as I can. I don't say to myself, 'You have to do this.' She does things, and I

4. From written notes in Dutch, Yolande Bertsch to Ogden and Erenstein, 11 February 1975.
5. From taped interview in English, Marja Kok with Ogden, 25 February 1975, Amsterdam. Transcribed by Gillian Bagwell.

give her a response, being more passive." This sort of insight reflects the quality of the role-building between the two actresses.

It should be clear by now that the Werkteater's role-building and playmaking depended on much more than theatrical improvisation. For one thing, the Werkteater actors were first-rate theatrical technicians—in voice, speech, gesture, movement, and timing. Their mastery of these skills enabled them to let technique become second nature, so that the artist in them could bring to the fore their own inner qualities. Despite all of the misreadings of Stanislavsky, this is precisely what he was driving at.

Voice and sound, sight and gestures are some of the ways and means of intercourse and transmission of the life of the spirit; moreover, these are far from being the best. Most often people communicate by invisible spiritual currents, an aura of feeling, a bidding of the will; this mode, from soul to soul, the most direct, spontaneously influencing, is the only mode for the transmission of the inexpressible, the supraconscious unyielding either to word or gesture. Living oneself, one compels others with whom one comes into contact to live. "You cry, if you want me to cry."

In his notes on theory—which he valued much more than the anecdotal *My Life in Art* demanded by his American publisher—Stanislavsky recognized "the power, the irresistibility and contagiousness" of emotional communication. "Its nature is still unsolved," he wrote, "but the force of its influence is known." He had devoted himself to resolving the central and terrible dilemma of the actor: "Our human nature cannot simultaneously live for itself, forgetting the spectator, and at the same time remember him and live on display." Stanislavsky saw the edge of the stage as "the fourth wall" and the members of the audience as sitting beyond it. Over and over again he admonished his actors to ignore the audience. The actors of the Werkteater, however, went further. They did adhere to many of Stanislavsky's ideals, but they broke down this fourth wall by actively including the spectators within their awareness while performing.[6]

6. Konstantin Stanislavsky, "First copy, Editional, K. Stanislavsky," trans. R. Lednicky and V. Wakeman, unpubl. MS (ca. 1923), 33, 128, 129, The Bancroft Library,

Their inner technique depends on real human bonds. In the dying scene Marja Kok and Yolande Bertsch establish strong bonds with each other. That becomes a primary inner quality, which the audience is drawn to imitate. What makes this capacity unusual, even among master actors, is that it springs from real-life ties that the actors have managed to form with each other. For many years the Werkteater actors consciously struggled to trust and accept each other in the matrix where daily life inevitably fuses with rehearsal and performance.

Shireen Strooker, who served as the stimulator for *Twilight*, described this personal commitment as follows. "The most important thing also in making a project is to dare to take the failures. You think: 'He disappoints me here, she's terrible there—the whole thing, it's a terrible situation. I don't know what to do with the play.'" She then compared a group project to a relationship with children. "You love a child, but the child becomes sick. Or the children hurt each other, and spoil everything you've just made, and don't eat. You can say, 'OK, I'm going to throw the child away and look for another child,' but you can also say, 'We're going through this phase together, and we'll come into a better phase after this.'" In the Werkteater, she said, "Everybody is absolutely different, and we use that. Because it's like life, like society: you have to live with each other."[7]

Human ties can become stronger when people play together; and firm ties forged between people outside the theater can enhance their playing with each other when they are inside the theater. Both of these dynamics occurred among Werkteater company members. That is, in their professional playing and playmaking they drew heavily on their personal friendships, jealousies, frictions, love affairs, and mundane worries. And because of these bonds with each other and with their roles, they

---

University of California, Berkeley. This is a collection of Stanislavsky's notes, which he intended to edit and publish as a core of his theory.

Of course, the notion of the front edge of the stage as "a fourth wall" originated with Diderot.

7. From taped interview in English, Shireen Strooker with Ogden, 22 February 1975, Soest (near Amsterdam). Transcribed by Gillian Bagwell.

could connect with their theatergoers during a performance. They would forge three links in a human chain, each dependent upon the preceding one: they connected with each other, which enabled them to connect with their roles, which finally enabled them to connect with their audiences.

To audience members, the openness, trust, and acceptance among Werkteater actors became quite evident, even when they put on stage their terrors in the face of dying. Since these attitudes are fundamental qualities that we want in our own daily lives, we are attracted to them in the theater. When we are in the presence of performers who exhibit these attitudes, we begin to identify with the performers, to imitate them—we experience a metamorphosis.

This dynamic presents drama schools with an important and often unrecognized challenge. During their major training period, actors must discover whether they are really capable of forming such close ties. Stanislavsky put his finger on the problem: "not everyone is endowed by nature to be able to live creatively and to recreate a role." And he defined "to live creatively" as to "live on the stage with living, genuine, and not actor's, emotions. The ability to experience is a natural gift, a talent, given from above to only a few."[8] For a mature actor, this capacity is as elementary as the ability to remember lines. Without it, there can be no real playing together, and therefore no *living* theater. And what good is live theater if it is not a playing together?

Marja once said of performing on stage, "I come into a sort of state of mind . . . it's not a character, it's a state of mind." In the metamorphosis that occurs in audience members, this is precisely what happens—they take on this "state of mind."

Marja said this about her partnership with Yolande: "We always say to each other when we do the scene, 'Just let it happen.' We have that confidence in each other, at that moment: Never be nervous about it or play-act something. Just be there and it happens. . . . In the real world, I think it doesn't matter

---

8. Stanislavsky, "First copy," 41–42.

who sits there. But in acting, yes, it does." If Yolande were to do the scene with someone else, "she wouldn't—as I wouldn't—have that confidence, so I think she'd act the part more, work at it more, rather than just be it." Here Marja went on to make an important distinction between life and the craft of acting: "Yolande has more confidence with me, not because she likes me, but because in that scene we understand each other. You know, we understand the essence of what's happening." She continued: "We never rehearsed a thing. We just talked about it and did it. What we decided on was to have a scene between two women where one is dying. When the one is dying, everything comes out. Like having a baby, for instance. You know, everything comes out. We talked about it for five minutes and we understood each other. [Both women have children.] I made a suggestion to Yolande, Yolande picked it up right away, and we did it."

Few people possess the continuing inventive spark and the rigorous discipline needed to work in this manner month after month for several years. At the time Marja and Yolande made these observations, they had given much thought to the way in which they connected their personal and theatrical lives. They could have come to engage in such penetrating self-analysis and mutual criticism only within a framework of continual acceptance of each other. On a long-term basis, and without a leader or a director, that kind of working relationship is very rare.

Of course, at the time Marja said, "We never rehearsed a thing," she and Yolande had been working together for three years. Not only that, but they had known each other as friends for some twenty years. On the one hand, Marja said that she does join the person of Yolande with the role: "I've known Yolande for a long time. So when she sits there [on stage], I get the emotion [for the scene] because I think she's going to die, that's all. I think of her as Yolande." On the other hand, she distinguishes between her personal life and art: "If in real life I saw Yolande sitting alone somewhere, and she was dying, or she had a terrible pain, I would do the same thing, I hope. I don't know whether Yolande would do it for me. You never know. This scene is not a realistic thing. We made it up, I think, because we've both had the experience of having a child."

While they perform, both Yolande and Marja think about an analogy with giving birth, another time when complete concentration is demanded. Marja said: "It's rather the same thing, I think—having a child and dying. You feel it that way, a bit. You have to give in. When you have a pain and you resist, the pain gets worse. What you do is, you don't resist the pain. But when I had a child, I couldn't do it. I thought, if I don't resist the pain, I will die. When you're playing, it's the same way. You have to give in."

What Marja calls her special "state of mind," Yolande describes this way: "In general throughout this scene I certainly want to make things clear for myself but often not too conscious. I prepare myself for the scene by trying to concentrate on being wholly open and blank toward everything that happens. That often gives me a chance to slip in somewhere."

If the audience begins to become like these actors, they first imitate the actors' attitude in joining with each other. When Yolande quotes Marja as saying that the purpose of this scene, she felt, was "to show something where one person [Marja] accepts everything from the other [Yolande] and through this genuinely 'helps' the other to be complete," we quickly understand that what we value highly in the theatrical event is something we value highly in the life event—a resilient playing together. And that is the key to the effectiveness of the Werkteater actors.

Theater is a dose of life, except that on stage good performers are more alive than others, and the onlookers want that aliveness. All performance of drama involves some illusion, and here Yolande is certainly not dying. Yet these actresses are really living, not faking a fundamental human moment in front of us. People in the audience long for the kind of confidence these actors have with each other. This desire increases a natural tendency to imitate others when in their presence. The onlookers start to take on what Marja called "a state of mind." As a consequence, the very metamorphosis that occurs in Yolande and in

Marja while they play this scene also begins to take place inside members of their audience.[9]

9. Whereas Joost Merloo concentrates primarily on contagion of rhythm in performance, in *The Dance*, Judith Lynne Hanna in her recent study, *The Performer-Audience Connection*, also includes the transfer of emotion. Part of her audience survey had to do with intentions as stated by dancers and responses as written by spectators at eight quite different dance performances. Hanna notes that "Nearly all respondents felt the same or a similar emotion to the one they perceived onstage." Her survey includes indications of "respondents perceiving boredom or eroticism onstage and feeling the same." The concerts where she undertook her audience research were produced in Washington, D.C., by the Smithsonian Institution Division of Performing Arts Dance Series: performances of American tap dance; a reconstruction of a Helen Tamiris piece by the Repertory Dance Theatre of Utah; a Kabuki dance by Sachiyo Ito; a classical Indian Kuchipudi dance by Indrani; works by the Philippine Dance Company of New York and a Kathakali Dance Company from Kerala, India; and contemporary pieces by Douglas Dunn and by Sage Cowles and Molly Davis. (Austin: University of Texas Press, 1983), 188.

6

Recognition

The Experience
of the Audience

Jacques Copeau, perhaps the most influential teacher-director in modern France, once wrote: "There will never be a new theater until the day comes when the individual in the audience murmurs in his heart and with his heart the same words spoken by the individual on the stage."[1] Throughout their productions the people of the Werkteater managed to create moments like this, when the audience is brought into harmonic vibration with the performers. The key to this dynamic lies in the spectator's act of recognition, which is not simply an act of sense perception but an act of re-knowing (re-cognition) or rediscovery. Through recognition an audience member connects what is on stage with something in his or her own past experience. Copeau, like the people at the Werkteater, saw a theatrical event as a communal gathering aimed at achieving an emotional harmony through a celebration of common human identity.

During the performance this re-knowing—when and if it happens—takes place within us as audience members in what might be called two waves. In the first wave we feel a particular or subjective recognition. Seeing an actor put a shoè on the foot of an old woman, as for example Joop Admiraal does in *You Are My Mother*, may give us a fleeting image of having done some-

---

1. Henri Ghéon, *The Art of the Theatre*, trans. by Adele M. Fiske (New York: Hill and Wang, 1961), 79. Fiske translates one expression here as "the man in the audience" instead of "the individual."

thing similar and reactivate the feeling that we had at that time. The image and feeling may strike us hard or only ripple the surface of our consciousness. In the second wave we experience a general or objective recognition that partakes of the archetypal: we feel connected with the collective unconscious, with the entire human community. It is this recognition, occurring in two waves, that brings about Copeau's ideal of harmony.

Copeau also tells us what it is about the theatrical event that can engender this recognition. Audience members gather in the theater, he says, "to satisfy a liking they have for living together, for experiencing human passions together, the delight of laughter and of poetry, brought about more by means of the stage than by life."[2] The stage heightens life and intensifies it. Peter Brook points to the same intensification when he observes that an audience "has come from a life outside the theater that is essentially repetitive to a special arena in which each moment is lived more clearly and more tensely." Brook also asks: What is left when a theatrical performance is over? What remains? Stage pictures from different productions come to him—an old man naked in a storm on a heath, two vagabonds waiting under a tree—and he declares that after the play's end "something in the mind burns."[3]

When spectators undergo this experience of recognition, the onstage event or figure takes on a personal meaning for them. When they watch the actor Frank Groothof whirl and glide in his wheelchair through a dance to the live music of a Chopin piano waltz (Figs. 22 and 23), for example, they receive a meaning that does not come as a didactic message, as it would in *Everyman* or a play by Brecht. Nor is life in a wheelchair presented as a symbol for some kind of spiritual or moral confinement. Instead, the meaning they find is the sort of profound personal revelation that Viktor Frankl refers to when he says, "I think the meaning of our existence is not invented by ourselves, but rather de-

2. Jacques Copeau, *Notes sur le métier de comédien* (Paris: Michel Brient, 1955), 38–39.

3. Peter Brook, *The Empty Space* (New York: Avon, 1969), 127, 123. Philip Auslander has recently pointed out this parallel between Copeau and Brook—"'Holy Theatre' and Catharsis," *Theatre Research International* 9, no. 1 (Spring 1984): 16–29. Brook's burnings in the mind are what in the dance Arlene Croce calls *Afterimages* (New York: Knopf, 1977).

tected."[4] Elsewhere, Frankl writes: "Reality presents itself always in the form of a specific concrete situation, and since each life situation is unique, it follows that also the meaning of a situation must be unique." Since meaning in this sense is unique, it is a matter of personal discovery. And when discovering meaning, Frankl says, "we are perceiving a possibility embedded in reality."[5] Frankl (who spent years in Nazi concentration camps) concludes: "Man is—by virtue of the self-transcendent quality of the human reality—basically concerned with reaching out beyond himself, be it toward a meaning to fulfill, or toward another human being lovingly to encounter."[6]

The actors of the Werkteater typically would lead an audience to recognition through humor and identification. For example, when exposing the sentimentality of the variety-show couple in *A Hot Summer Night* (see Fig. 31), they make us see ourselves in them. Brecht would have done just the opposite: he would have made us despise them. The Werkteater actors did not aim to shock their audiences. They sought contact rather than confrontation, intimacy rather than alienation. Their pursuit of these goals—and the personal revelation they may bring—is well served by their emphasis on keeping the actor in steady contact with the audience. In this chapter we shall examine scenes from several Werkteater productions in order to discover just how they engendered this sort of personal recognition.

In the Werkteater's production of *Waldeslust*, a group of Dutch tourists is waiting in an airport lobby for their final travel arrangements to be made; they are going to Spain. When put in the theater, that very familiar scene becomes something new— something unfamiliar—so that we look again, and thereby discover some personal meaning in it. In the Werkteater production the scenes with tourists are juxtaposed with scenes of handicapped persons (see Figs. 34, 35). The handicapped are unfamiliar to most of us, but somewhere during the course of the

4. Viktor Frankl, *Man's Search for Meaning* (New York: Simon and Schuster, 1963), 157.
5. Viktor Frankl, *The Unheard Cry for Meaning* (New York: Simon and Schuster, 1978), 37–38.
6. Frankl, *The Unheard Cry*, 72, 80.

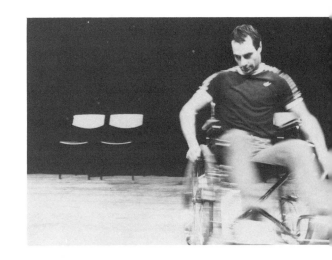

FIGURES 22 and 23.
Revelation and the
question of meaning.
If you live in a
wheelchair, you are
an acrobat. Audience
and Frank Groothof
in *Waldeslust*,
1980–81.

performance we realize that they have become familiar. Such a moment of recognition—and there are many in this play—first surprises us and then brings an inner delight.

The spontaneous laughter of delight is one expression of recognition. René Groothof's scene at the opening of *Waldeslust* provides a simple example. Here is a description of the whole scene, as performed on 13 June 1981, at the Academy of Fine Arts in Cologne, Germany. Many members of the audience, knowing that the piece would be about retarded people, were somewhat apprehensive about what they might see.

TIME

0:00   René, a rather clownish looking person with hair combed forward and wearing a red windbreaker, appears alone on stage. He could be in his twenties; he could be slightly retarded. He gives a big smile to the audience. He sits somewhat behind and to one side of a drum set. He is grinning, curious about the drum set. He looks at the audience, wanting the audience to see what he sees. He gets up, and from his movements and gestures we know that he is retarded.

0:30   He goes over and hits a cymbal with his hand. Clang. With a big smile he gives a thumbs-up sign to the audience. *The audience laughs slightly.*

0:45   He hits the other cymbal with his hand and again gives his thumbs-up sign to the audience. *The audience laughs slightly.* He points to the cymbal, looking at the audience. Then he taps the snare drum with his fingers.

1:00   René says something into the microphone standing at the drum set. It sounds like, "Geht nicht. Geht nicht." ["Doesn't work. Doesn't work."] It is the speech of a retarded person. Then twice he says into the microphone, "Kaput." He gives a big smile.

1:15   René sits down at the drum set, hesitates, and then steps hard on the foot pedal of the big drum. Thump—and he leaps up, startled. *The audience gives a bigger laugh and applauds sporadically.*

1:30   He sits down again at the drum set, and with his foot he thumps the big drum three, four, five times. He gives a thumbs-up sign to the audience.

1:40   His thumping becomes rhythmic. He picks up a drumstick,

1:50   and hits a snare drum—with one stick, then with two sticks simultaneously, continuing the rhythm, pounding like a child, raising the pair of sticks above his head at each blow.

2:00   He starts using the drumsticks alternately, like an accomplished drummer, continuing to thump with his foot and evolving an insistent jazz beat.

2:15   By now he has developed a rhythmic use of the whole drum set, like a jazz drummer. He gives a big smile: he can do it! (See Fig. 24.) *The audience applauds loudly and laughs.* Other musicians appear, and with René laying down the beat, the music for the show begins. Later on René will play a retarded person in a number of the scenes.

With his smile and his thumbs-up sign, René has invited the audience into his discovery. He has signaled to them that he is OK. If the audience members are apprehensive, his smile and thumbs-up sign give them permission to laugh. In the live theater, it is laughing *with* the actor that we most prize, for it brings us into unexpected harmony with the imperfect human nature we see on stage.

René's timing and his structuring of the scene are impressive. After a buildup in which he engages the curiosity of the audience with his own interest in the drum set, a sudden cymbal clang and his thumbs-up gesture release the audience's laughter of recognition. This occurs again. In the third laugh, released by the thump of the bass drum and René's sudden jump, we in the audience find ourselves identifying with him. We too are startled. Then, over the next forty-five seconds, there is another buildup. René begins to look and sound more and more like a real drummer, setting up an infectious beat as he proceeds. And to his pure delight, it dawns on him that maybe he can really take command. Can he? We in the audience, though already charmed by his childlike manner and his open smile, have considered him incapable. Now we are rooting for him. He is the underdog, trying to do something we have all dreamed of doing: walking up to an unfamiliar instrument and discovering, suddenly, that we can play it. When René's beat becomes triumphant and his joy unbounded (see Fig. 24), the audience breaks into its loudest laughter and applauds his achievement. At that moment René has made a happy discovery, and so have we, for the act of recognition itself gives us pleasure.

When the Werkteater decided to experiment by producing a traditional drama, after nearly a decade of creating their own plays, it was natural for them to turn to Chekhov. More than any other playwright, Chekhov introduced audiences of the twentieth century to the experience of recognition in the theater, the deep pleasure of seeing themselves with fresh eyes. When staging Chekhov's *Uncle Vanya*, however, the actors of the Werkteater kept to their own style. In their hands, Chekhov's Russian estate became not a quaint and faraway place but a thoroughly familiar setting: the Werkteater's bare playing space with a table, a trellis, and a swing. The dress used by the actors was also spare and contemporary (Fig. 25). Hans Man in't Veld later said: "For an audience member, it was as if you had come to these people for a visit. Very intimate. You were very close to the actors. There was a lot of laughter."[7]

These examples begin to reveal the Werkteater's basic means of bringing audience members to an inner recognition. Either the actors would take something unfamiliar, such as the Russian estate in *Uncle Vanya* or the retarded drummer in *Waldeslust*, and then they would make it familiar; or they would choose something very commonplace to us and make it unfamiliar.

In his one-man show *You Are My Mother*, Joop Admiraal plays both himself and his own mother.[8] As the performance starts,

7. Interview in English, Hans Man in't Veld with Ogden, 14 May 1982, Amsterdam.
8. Joop Admiraal, *U bent mijn moeder* (Amsterdam: International Theater Bookshop, 1982). Also in German: *Du bist meine Mutter* (Amsterdam: International Theater Bookshop, 1983).

FIGURE 24. He can
do it! Laughter at
the moment of discovery.
René Groothof hammers
the drum in *Waldeslust*,
1981.

FIGURE 25.
Experiment with a traditional role.
Joop Admiraal as Astrov,
in *Uncle Vanya* by Chekhov,
Werkteater production, 1979.

Joop sits stage right at a table. After a bit he gets up, carries some flowers across to an empty bed stage left, and tells us in the audience that he is going for his Sunday visit to his mother in an old people's home. He is dressed in a suit. He sits on the edge of the bed and begins talking with the imagined woman, speaking first with his own voice and then with the quavering older voice of his mother.

Before our eyes the familiar begins to become unfamiliar. Joop says that he will help his mother to dress and then take her out for her walk. He pulls off his jacket, shoes, and pants. Underneath he has on a slip and stockings. He puts on a pair of women's glasses. Still on the edge of the bed, he turns to the audience, growing now rather stiff and bent. At this moment the audience sees Joop as the old woman laboring to get into a blouse and skirt. The conversation continues. The mother bends over to shove her feet into her shoes. A stockinged foot pushes spasmodically at a shoe, the muscles twitching. The foot will not go in. Then the firm hands of the son grasp the foot and the shoe, push the one into the other, and do up the buckle (Fig. 26).

The old woman now struggles to her feet (Fig. 27). From Joop we continue to hear the two voices in conversation, as mother and son take a walk, but the predominant physical presence is that of an old woman. The performance ends as it began, with Joop standing and moving as a man, talking with the imagined woman lying in her bed. "Mother, I have made a play about you and me," he says to her, "and now there's a scene at the end where you say you don't want to live anymore." But dying—he concludes the performance—"It isn't that easy. You are still living." Joop is calling attention here to the relationship between his life and his play.

Many of the details of gesture and language that Joop the actor-playwright uses during this performance recall familiar episodes in our own lives. Yet because Joop, a man, plays the mother as well as himself, the familiar elements are made unfamiliar, and this enables us to perceive moments from our own child-parent relationships in a new and profoundly personal light.

By playing both his mother and himself, and by confronting

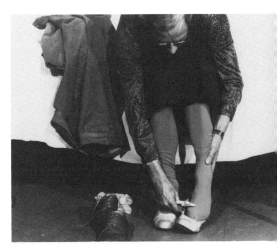

FIGURES 26 and 27.
Recognition: the familiar
is made unfamiliar.
Joop Admiraal playing himself
and his own mother in
You Are My Mother, 1981.

his mother's living and dying in an attitude of play, Joop assumes the existential position of *homo ludens*—the human being as player in the theater of life—and therefore induces members of his audience to see their own child-parent relationships from that perspective. At the same time Joop's production induces in members of his audience a Zen-like attitude of inward concentration and meditation, one of mindfulness and self-possession. This is also what Marja and Yolande do at the end of *Twilight*. While thinking of themselves in the play as older women, which they are not, they are reaching out to each other through the intimate bonds of their real friendship; and as they deal on stage with the physical process of dying, which they have not experienced in person, they are imagining the physical process of giving birth, which they have.[9]

In *A Hot Summer Night*, one of the Werkteater's summer tent productions, Gerard Thoolen plays a black woman from Surinam (Figs. 28 and 29). The strangeness of such a person to European and American audiences is exaggerated by the fact that she is played by a man in blackface. The comedy is a zany piece about a traveling variety show run by a Dutch family. When a Surinamese woman appears in the backstage area, delivering a telephone order of her homemade shish kebabs, the old father insults her to her face: she is fat and stupid, a peddler of rotten meat, a welfare cheat living off the money of honest taxpayers. He loathes blacks. He is a comic stereotype of the bigot, whose suspicion and hate spring from a fear of the unknown. But she, also a comic stereotype, takes everything with grace and a great laugh.

During the course of the play, this odd figure of a woman becomes familiar to us, just as she becomes familiar to the old father. We come to know her because she, like all of us, has a breaking point: she can take only so much. Still full of zest and good humor, she participates in the variety show's fox-trot contest, until suddenly she trips and falls. The dance music stops,

9. In Artaud's terms the experience that we share with Marja and Yolande conjures up a Dance of Death, and our experience with Joop conjures up a Double of Parent-Child, an archetypal image of Age-Youth.

and there is silence. Then, sitting there sprawled on the floor in front of the tent crowd, she reaches over, picks up the microphone, and begins to sing a dark and haunting spiritual.

This role contains an essence of Werkteater comedy, for the Surinamese woman, Mrs. Emanuels, is both funny and tragic. When she starts to sing, we recognize her humanity. She is a displaced person, and the contrast between her early song about coconuts and her later spiritual reveals her as caught between two cultures—the Dutch culture she must now cope with and the Surinamese culture of her youth. At this moment in her life, however, she amalgamates the two, singing in the words of her spiritual that she can be happy anywhere. On the surface she is all laughter, while deep inside she embraces the disparities of human life. In her person, comedy and tragedy fuse. At the conclusion of the play, when she sits before us as a mother-slave holding the show owners' baby, we recognize and share some feeling of the huge contrasts she embodies (Fig. 30). By underscoring the unfamiliar at first, the actors of the Werkteater fascinate us and make us look again. Then they dispel our fear of the unknown so that we can see into the heart of a character.

What happens when Gerard plays the Surinamese woman happened frequently in Werkteater productions, both those that were filled with laughter and those that were not. *Waldeslust* gives us that experience with the retarded drummer. In *Twilight* the actor Peter Faber says that the potentially dreadful and unfamiliar business of entering an old people's home feels to him like his first day in school. Dying is shown in *Twilight*, but that necessarily unfamiliar experience is treated by the actors as analogous to the process of giving birth, something familiar to the two of them—a situation in which one lets go and the other takes care of her. In *Glasses and Braces*, a production for children, the actors romp around in scenes that actively deal with children's fears. By using theatrical elements to accentuate the unfamiliar and then transforming it into something familiar, the actors impel us to discover some new meaning for ourselves. Many great nonrealistic plays, such as those by Shakespeare, work in this way.

FIGURE 28.
Film, 1981.

Recognition: the unfamiliar is made familiar.
Gerard Thoolen as the Surinamese woman,
Mrs. Emanuels, in *A Hot Summer Night*.

FIGURE 29. Summer production
in the tent, 1978–79.

FIGURE 30. Recognition: the unfamiliar
is made familiar. Gerard Thoolen
as the Surinamese woman, Mrs. Emanuels,
with Joop Admiraal as baby,
in *A Hot Summer Night*. Film, 1981.

In order to reach levels of experience that lie beneath the surface of familiar actions, the player-playwright must create mimetic poetry, poetry specifically for the stage. In a Sophoclean or Shakespearian speech the word is made special, and in poetry for the eye, as in the dance, the gesture is made special. Both types of mimetic poetry occur in the performance of drama at its best.

In the theater successful mimetic poetry requires more than techniques of language and movement. The atmosphere must be right. The audience must be ready to sit and pay attention, and the performer must be ready to call their attention to what he or she says and does. Both actor and audience member know that what will happen is theater, not life. Mimetic poetry is not part of life outside the theater; it can occur only when people witness actions being presented with deliberate craft on stage.

In *You Are My Mother* the audience sees a commonplace episode masterfully executed and heightened. The word *heightened* here means "made unfamiliar." When Joop plays two roles almost simultaneously, his normal everyday words and sentences take on uncommon shapes. They become distilled, charged with meaning. Japanese haiku achieves this effect in part by restricting itself to very few words. By the same token, when he dresses himself as an old woman, Joop creates visual poetry from a banal activity by focusing our attention on its rhythms and physical details—something that modern dance often does.

At the most fundamental level, what Joop Admiraal does on stage is call our attention to qualities of the moment. He intrigues us, and so we look closely. And therein lies an important key to the impact of the Werkteater actors: they would take common things in life and make them fascinating to an audience. To paraphrase W. B. Yeats's definition of the poet, when Joop performs the ordinary act of helping his mother put on her shoes, he makes the unseen seen, and the unheard heard. At the end of the play, when Joop says to his mother that dying "isn't that easy," the line itself is banal. But in the context of his performance, it has the impact of great poetry.

7

Seven
Characteristics
of the
Werkteater

A Summary

As a major actors' theater, the Werkteater exhibited important practices and results that provide a standard against which other groups can measure themselves. Here we shall summarize the chief characteristics of the Werkteater during its growth and maturity, under seven headings.

Primacy of the Actor

The members of the Werkteater began a theater revolution in Holland in 1970 by placing their emphasis on the actor. That emphasis, which remained intact 1970–85, is the source of all the other characteristics we shall describe.

All original members of the Werkteater—the 1970 founders, together with Joop (1972), Olga (1974), Frank (1974), and René (1980)—have the mysterious and magnetic quality we call *presence*. No one knows what creates it, but everyone recognizes it. At a drama school, for example, one may see the work of a hundred students on the stage before coming across someone with real presence. Consciously and unconsciously, the people who started the Werkteater banded together because they recognized this quality in each other, and over the years they recruited others who have it. When I would ask close observers from outside the company what one quality above all others singles out a Werkteater actor, most of them would say "presence."

As we have noted, the Werkteater actors were not beginners. They had been trained in drama schools and had solid experience in professional theater. It took two years for them to come to know and trust each other. In order to stay together, they needed a great deal of professional help, and the process was painful. The actors who remained were those who were willing to dive deep within themselves, to abandon all personal pretense and fakery, and to commit themselves to working as team players over a period of years. In this they were unusual. Many a skilled actor simply cannot cooperate in a group as an equal among equals on a long-term basis.

At the same time each of the Werkteater actors has an uncommonly strong drive to invent—in daily improvisations, rehearsals, and performances. When I would ask the actors themselves what one quality above all others singles out a Werkteater actor, most company members would say "inventiveness." This quality, too, is unusual. Over the long run most actors are probably more comfortable with learning written lines and taking guidance from a director.

Linked to this inventiveness is a will to continue training. Throughout the years, for instance, the group maintained a regimen of acrobatic exercises with professional acrobats, which they used as much for physical conditioning and balance as for display. When they did engage in acrobatic stunts during a production, they staged them intentionally to convey a sense of fun and homeliness. Figure 31, a photograph of the husband-and-wife variety show team in *A Hot Summer Night*, makes the point. The actors would take up other forms of training—singing, dancing, mime, yoga, and special voice work—according to the demands of the piece they were evolving at the moment.

Scrupulous attention to nuances of facial and bodily expression prepared members of the company for the kind of close camera work that we value in films and television (Figs. 32 and 33). Sustained intimacy with audiences in their stage productions, as in *Twilight* and *A Hot Summer Night*, readied them for the intimacy of a film studio. Even the ways in which they would go about constructing a play resemble the ways in which motion picture people often make their films—from day to day they work on the scenes while performing them. In fact, the Werkteater company is one of the few companies that have crossed the bridge from stage to screen with overwhelming success. In 1980, with a piece called *In for Treatment*, they came out of nowhere, as far as the television world knew, to win the Prix d'Italia, the international grand prize for television drama. They had been together for a decade, but it was their first full-scale attempt at television performance.

Playmaking Through Playing

As playwrights—craftsmen who make plays, as shipwrights once made ships—the Werkteater actors connected themselves totally with the roles they performed. Because they are actors, their plays have an organic connection with the living dynamics of the stage—rhythms of performance, timing, theatrical effect, sound, visual and vocal emphasis, and moment-by-moment relationship with audiences. They are like pianists who compose for the piano, or dancers who choreograph for the stage.

The log of *Twilight* has described how playmaking at the Werkteater would proceed. The actors developed a piece primarily through improvisation, coupled with the use of relevant source material from life—such as consultations with people from intended audiences. Their approach to the chosen subject, whether a serious examination of aging, as in *Twilight*, or a farcical treatment of marriage, as in *A Hot Summer Night*, would grow out of the actor's inner self. As a result, the subject always

Stage methods
match film and
television methods.

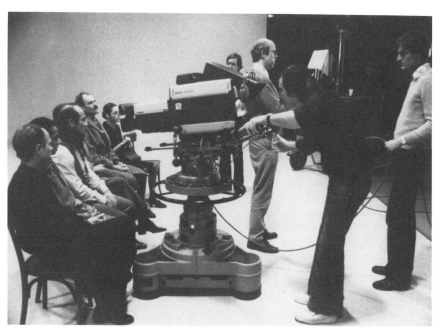

had to do with the human condition. That is why the dynamic of recognition is so significant in their work.

To achieve this recognition they built many of their dramatic structures on the principle of contrast. For example, when developing *Waldeslust*, the actors divided up and worked in two separate clusters. In the resulting performance, scenes of Dutch tourists flying to Spain for a holiday, evolved by one cluster, were alternated with scenes of handicapped people, evolved by the other (Figs. 34 and 35). On stage the two groups never meet. But just as insights came to the actors while they were constructing the play in this fashion, so insights came to the audiences as they watched it.

This same process of developing insights marks *Hello Fellow*, which presents a clash between the world of several middle-class ladies suddenly smitten with egalitarian feelings and the world of the street people they patronizingly invite to tea. Each world lives by its own rules, and goodwill is simply not enough to bring them together. Opposition as a technique becomes apparent in the way the Werkteater playwrights use many of their characters. In *Twilight* they bring a young schoolgirl into a home for the elderly. In *A Hot Summer Night* they contrast the mean-spirited old show-business father with the lighthearted Surinamese woman, and the strained marriage of two vigorous vaudevillians (see Fig. 31) with the hopeless marriage of a dull bureaucrat and a volatile alcoholic (see Fig. 39).

Opposition generates tension: inner tension of character, outer tension between characters, and tension within a scene and between scenes, as one contrasts with the next. Such opposition is a fundamental element of dramaturgy. For example, when we analyze the causes of laughter in the theater, we can be certain of only three ingredients: atmosphere, contrast or opposition, and distance. Or, we might refer to the three elements as a mood for laughing, an opposition that sparks it, and a safe remove from the action. For the audience, in the end, it is as much the resolution of tension that leads to revelation as it is revelation that releases tension.

The source of this principle of opposition lies within each

Playing through playmaking.
Tourist scenes contrast
with scenes between
handicapped people
in *Waldeslust*, 1981.

FIGURE 34.
The tourists, left
to right: Joop Admiraal,
Daria Mohr, Kees Prins,
Hans Man in't Veld,
and Cas Enklaar.

FIGURE 35.
The handicapped:
Marja Kok and
Frank Groothof.

actor as an individual. In the first place, all Werkteater company members had had special training in another art or craft—in singing or playing a musical instrument, in painting, sculpture, or design, and in dance, mime, or athletics—so that during a performance at least two sides of an actor would become visible.

At a deeper level the members of the Werkteater would find dramatic contrast by staging the personal contradictions within themselves. In *You Are My Mother,* for instance, the contrast derives from the solo actor's switching back and forth between his own inner qualities of the masculine and the feminine, the son and the mother whom he carries within him. This constant use of their own paradoxes kept the actors fresh and prevented them from stagnating in clichés.

If *plot*, a sequence of episodes usually marked by contrast, is their means of storytelling, what then is *character?* The word itself reflects the poverty of our language for theatrical analysis. Who are *dramatis personae?* Joop as his mother? Gerard as a Surinamese woman? René as a retarded drummer? Marja and Helmert as a variety show couple? As Marja said in discussing her role in *Twilight*, what these actors play is not a character but a state of mind.[1] Commenting on his role as an old man in *Twilight*, Herman also talks about an attitude or an inner condition:

In many plays about old people, I see the actor imitating a little old man. Well, I don't really think about playing an old man. I just try to investigate constantly what it would mean to me to be old—during the play. There's a process going on all the time, exactly the same as in life. And that's the different thing about playing a part in Shakespeare, for example: then, this process is going on only during rehearsals, where

1. From taped interview in English, Marja Kok with Ogden, 25 February 1975, Amsterdam. Transcribed by Gillian Bagwell.

From a semioticist's point of view, Marco de Marinis has shown recently how the spectator takes charge of the assignment of meaning to a performance and, in a sense, becomes the protagonist of the drama. *Semiotica del teatro. L'analisi testuale dello spettacolo* (Milan: Bompiani, 1982). For an English translation of an excerpt, see de Marinis, "Theatrical Comprehension: A Socio-Semiotic Approach," *Theater* 15, no. 1 (Winter 1983): 12–17. For a discussion of the spectator's identification with the performer and with the dramatic character, see "Passies in pluche, de toeschouwer in de hoofdrol," transcription of a lecture by Henri Schoenmakers (Utrecht: Instituut voor Theaterwetenschap, Rijksuniversiteit Utrecht, 1986).

you start from a concept and try to fill it in, to make it correspond with yourself as an actor and as a human being.[2]

The members of the Werkteater extended even further this practice of matching process with product: they never regarded a play in public performance as finished. The time of development might range from three months to nine months or a year, as with *Twilight*. Then, while a piece was being presented to audiences on a regular basis, the actors would continually change it. They would exchange roles, drop major sequences, and try out wholly new material. Only their commitment to long-term ensemble work made this practice possible.

The Use of a Stimulator

When the Werkteater actors came together in 1970, they shared a desire to escape what they called the tyranny of the director. During their second year they discovered the notion of the stimulator. At the outset in the evolution of a new project, one of the actors would take the job of stimulator. Shireen did this for *Twilight*. She convened discussions. She went to different groups of actors as they worked on improvisations in order to give them suggestions and to point out things that seemed promising and things that did not. And she led in the process of pruning and shaping the material into a whole performance. Shireen also took two different acting roles in *Twilight* at two different times during the years it remained in the repertory.

Each stimulator would function in a way that suited his or her own personality. One might work a bit more as a coach, another more as an editor, another more as a resource person. Often the original idea for a project would come from the actor who would become the stimulator. While serving as the stimulator, this actor—unlike a traditional stage director—would con-

---

2. From taped interview in English, Herman Vinck with Ogden, 13 April 1975, Amsterdam. Transcribed by Gillian Bagwell.

tinually play in other pieces, some in early phases of development and others in front of audiences. Thus the Werkteater's
primary emphasis on the actor carried through the stimulator,
who brought an actor's sensibilities to the project, and who continued to act in other projects and thus did not become separated from the cast. Moreover, the stimulator's own acting was
enriched by working as a stimulator.[3]

Long Experience Together

To function as a creative instrument the company had to stay together for many years. This characteristic has marked almost all
great acting companies in the past, as it has marked great cham-
ber music ensembles. It is an experience that has shaped profoundly both the personal and professional patterns of Werkteater actors, both their inner and their outer lives.

We have already seen that the effort to keep the company
intact posed a formidable challenge to the actors personally, as
individuals. At times the Werkteater as a group called upon a
psychiatrist or a psychologist for assistance. Some members left
and then came back. But the struggle was always a collective one.

Many of the deeper qualities of Werkteater performances
grew directly out of the hardships the actors endured in order
to remain a cohesive group. Dealing with insult, maintaining
dignity under stress, and accepting individual differences in the
midst of individual conflict—these very personal struggles
brought emotional truth to their productions. For example,
while we laugh, we recognize the generosity of spirit in the Surinamese woman as she turns aside the insults of the old father in
A Hot Summer Night—until she can take no more. And in the
last scene in Twilight we recognize both Yolande's drive to hold

3. For a monograph devoted to Shireen Strooker's work as a stimulator, see Dunbar H.
Ogden's Actor Training and Audience Response (Berkeley and Fresno: The Oak
House, 1984). This volume contains a record of two performance projects developed by Shireen Strooker with students at the University of California, Berkeley:
illustrations of Werkteater techniques, evaluations by the trainees, and responses
by audiences to those parts of the work that were shown publicly.

on to her dignity as she dies and Marja's growing acceptance of her, as by chance she comes along at that moment and chooses to take care of Yolande.

Variety in Kinds of Performance

The members of the company always attempted new projects with each other under new conditions. These forms ranged from children's pieces to a few productions of a script, such as *The Caretaker* and *Uncle Vanya*. As with all their projects, each of these dramas was chosen primarily in order to introduce a very particular element at a very particular time into the mosaic of the company's existing work. Contrasting types of projects allowed the performers not only to explore different moods but also to experience different periods of project development. For example, the company put together their farce *Menotti* in only three weeks and ran it for only a couple of months. Variety of performance would also permit the actors to work in different combinations with each other: Joop's one-man show of *You Are My Mother*, the two-woman show *Marja and Shireen*, and the nearly full-company production of *Twilight*. Variety here meant stretch, risk, and renewal for the actor.

An Intimate Playing Space

The actors preferred to perform under close actor-audience conditions, not in proscenium theaters. The company's own theater was a large room in a renovated factory in downtown Amsterdam. For most productions a rectangular playing space was defined by the audience's 150 movable chairs, some of which were on risers, and by the actors' risers, occasionally with tables and chairs.

Figures 1 and 36 show how near the actors were to their audiences and the importance they would place on facial expression. To concentrate on essentials in the act of recognition, they

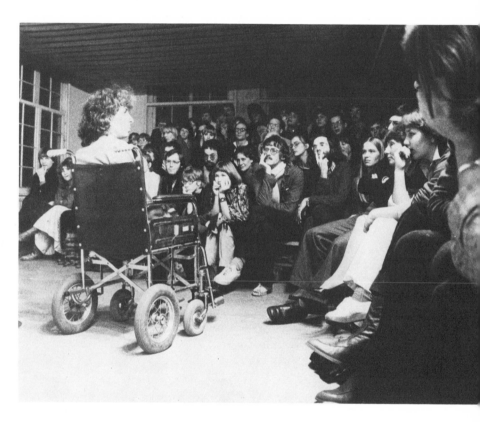

FIGURE 36. An intimate playing space.
Shireen Strooker and audience in
Werkteater's regular theater.
Performance of *Scared to Death*, 1978–79.

tended to omit scenery and props. Many of their performances also took place in intimate settings outside their theater, such as the halls and lounges of schools and various other institutions. As of the late 1970s their popularity led them to use a tent designed by Herman Vinck, in which they could seat 750 persons for their summer shows. Yet even here, the audience surrounded 270 degrees of a central playing area, and a spectator in the back row sat no more than thirty-seven feet from the center.

For an actor, a performance space serves as a comrade or as an opponent. It is therefore out of a working sensitivity to their environment that the Werkteater troupe would seek out and construct spaces that supported rather than endangered their emphasis on the actor and their desire for intimate contact with their audiences.

Steady Contact with the Audience

The company's continual interaction with their playgoers applied to their processes of play development as well as to their processes of performance. Their *KLM Project*, for example, which dealt with human relations in the business world, was produced in the offices of KLM, the Dutch national airline. After the performance (Fig. 37), they broke up into small discussion groups, each actor with some of the airline's personnel (Fig. 38). Shortly thereafter the actors performed again, this time using suggestions they had received from this audience. Sometimes after a performance in an institution they would introduce discussion, and occasionally they would follow the discussion immediately with improvisations based on spectators' reactions. This contact would tell performers as performers when they were honest and when they were dishonest, when they were on the mark and when they were off the mark. It both stimulated them and kept them human.

The practice of holding Evening Workshops, at which specific groups were invited to watch and then discuss an evolving production with the actors, began in the 1971–72 season and

Steady contact with the audience.

FIGURES 37, 38.
Performance followed by discussion.
KLM Project, a series with
KLM Airline personnel, 1972.
Actors (above), left to right:
Yolande Bertsch, Herman Vinck,
Cas Enklaar, Rense Royaards,
Hans Man in't Veld, Joop Admiraal,
Helmert Woudenberg, Peter Faber,
and Gerard Thoolen.

since then became standard for the troupe. When developing *Twilight*, the company also performed in homes for the elderly and then modified the piece to reflect their experiences there. Thus, in his comments on the text, Herman speaks of meeting in a home an old man very much like the character he was developing for himself: a man who liked to work with his hands, who took great pride in his craftsmanship with wood. This man's practices and attitudes reinforced Herman's evolving role in the play. Even more specifically, Peter describes how after months of work he finally discovered the key to his role in two sentences spoken to him by one of these senior citizens: "To be old is bad; to get old is not. I'm not afraid of getting old; I'm afraid to *be* old." The man was eighty-six. Peter began to use these very sentences in his performance. According to the actors, what they wanted to get from the discussions with audiences that often followed regular performances was not praise for their abilities but rather an expression of personal feeling or remembered experience, a revealing of genuine recognition on the part of the playgoer.

Finally, in their performance style itself the actors would both give to and draw from their audiences. They accomplished this either by addressing the spectators directly or, more commonly, by internally opening themselves up to the spectators while playing with each other. All Werkteater performances would slip constantly back and forth between explicit and implicit encounter with the audience.

In our time we have made a kind of idol of self-expression, and nowhere do we find more worshippers of it than in the theater—and no wonder, since the actor must work relentlessly on himself, the most difficult instrument of expression in the world. Yet the urgency of full-blooded contact with their audiences over the years did sometimes push members of the Werkteater beyond self-expression into what Viktor Frankl calls "true encounter," an experience "based on self-transcendence rather than mere self-expression."[4]

4. Viktor Frankl, *The Unheard Cry for Meaning* (New York: Simon and Schuster, 1978), 72, 80.

8

Theater
for Tomorrow

———

The past illuminates the present, and the present may point to the future. But in this case, how? Looking back, we can see that the Werkteater has much in common with commedia dell'arte companies, such as those of the internationally famous Andreini family and the company headed by Giuseppe Biancolelli, which was the favorite of Louis XIV. Like these troupes, the Werkteater had about a dozen players, each of them with special talents. The Amsterdam company had no stars, however, because its work demanded intimate cooperation, and on stage each actor had to concentrate intensely on what was happening. Both commedia dell'arte and the Werkteater started with only a rough scenario, though a Werkteater scenario was thoroughly fleshed out before performance. Both were troupes of traveling comedians and used theatrical devices that are strikingly similar.

In *A Hot Summer Night*, for example, Hans and Olga and Rense—playing a local bureaucrat, his wife, and his son—sit among the theatergoers (Fig. 39). For theatrical fun, Rense, a man in his thirties, plays the adolescent son. *A Hot Summer Night* is about a family-run variety show that travels from town to town and performs in a tent—which is exactly what the Werkteater actors were doing at the moment. Every year they would develop a new farce and tour with it during the summer months through the cities and villages of Holland (Fig. 40).

At the Werkteater, life and art were always converging, as

they might have done in the great commedia dell'arte troupes as well. The Werkteater actors put their own comic lives on stage, and they designed their performances for the communities to which they would go. For example, when their own group experience led them to develop a piece such as *Good Morning, Sir,* which deals with the lives of office workers, they played it especially for businesspeople, sometimes during the lunch break in an office building (Figs. 41 and 42). We recall, incidentally, that master-servant relationships, the medieval and Renaissance equivalent of employer-employee interactions, were a favorite theme in commedia performances. After performing their play, the Werkteater actors would mingle with the officeworkers and invite feedback—what parts rang true, what parts did not? Their desire to find out, as always, was both personal and artistic, because their themes in this piece—the individual versus the group, isolation versus fellowship—expressed their own experiences in working together.

But for historical parallels to the Werkteater's deeper revelations about the truth of the human condition, we must look to the troupes of Shakespeare and Molière, for whom the achievement of depth could be even more difficult in comedy than it was in tragedy. To a significant degree, it was the life-style or work-style of those actors in the sixteenth and seventeenth centuries that made possible the complex works of Shakespeare and Molière, playwrights who were themselves actors. In those companies the actors started out young, and the few who stayed on, unable to live without the company, played together for years— Shakespeare's actors for nearly two decades and Molière's for nearly three. Indeed the ideal way of learning how to play Shakespeare and Molière would be for a company to begin by making its own plays. The process of creating a theater piece from scratch forces the members of an ensemble to risk more, to clarify more, to function more as a team, to understand themselves better, and to take personal responsibility for every aspect of the play.

Jacques Copeau has provided a modern example of this process and what its results could be. In 1924 he took his young company away from Paris to his native Burgundy, where they trained

They are really traveling comedians.

FIGURE 39.
Actors as audience.
An adult plays a child.
Rense Royaards (with toy dog),
Hans Man in't Veld and
Olga Zuiderhoek (in tuxedo
and evening dress) in
A Hot Summer Night.
Summer production
in the tent, 1978–79.

FIGURE 40.
The Werkteater's summer-production
tent in the Dutch town
of Middelburg, 1974.

Life and art constantly converge.
Performance of *Good Morning, Sir,*
in an office building in
the Dutch town of Amersfoort,
1974.

FIGURE 41.
Actors, left to right:
Gerard Thoolen, Helmert Woudenberg,
Frank Groothof, Rense Royaards,
Cas Enklaar, Peter Faber,
and Hans Man in't Veld.

FIGURE 42. Actors:
(left row) Gerard Thoolen
and Rense Royaards; (center row)
Joop Admiraal, Helmert Woudenberg,
Cas Enklaar, and Hans Man in't Veld;
(right row) Frank Groothof
and Peter Faber.

as "les Copiaus" and only occasionally produced plays. In their training during the next four years they often used methods of playmaking. In 1929 a core of Copeau's actors carried his influence directly into the formation the Compagnie des Quinze, under the leadership of Copeau's nephew and collaborator Michel Saint-Denis. Copeau combined the use of improvisational techniques (among others) with a reverence for the literary text. Throughout his life, for example, he drew particular inspiration from the comedies of Molière and Shakespeare (especially *Twelfth Night* and *As You Like It*). Through his training and directing he developed in his actors uncommon skills in diction, gesture, mime, and movement; and he also imparted to them his own almost religious sense of the playwright-actor-audience relationship. As a result, no group of actors has shaped contemporary French theater more profoundly than Copeau's.

Jac Heijer, the Dutch theater critic, has rightly observed that "drama writers, critics, and, in recent times, directors, have always understood each other rather well," but that the problem person in the enterprise has always been the actor: "performer and critic, for example, are continually falling into conflict."[1] It is significant, I think, that in seeking a renewal of theater, the actors of the Werkteater almost instinctively avoided directors and critics. As commedia players did, they went directly to audiences, especially nontheatrical audiences. And like Shakespeare and Molière, they began with the processes of a working company. More playmaking in the future may begin not with a script but with a method. We may see fewer new dramas and more schools of actors with special themes, companies akin to our present dance troupes, jazz ensembles, and performance-art groups.

The parallels between the Werkteater, the commedia actors, and the companies of Shakespeare and Molière also tell us something about the natural life cycle of a troupe, which like any living organism has a youth, a middle age, and an old age. In the twentieth century few companies have managed to grow beyond youth, but among those that have—such as the troupes led by

1. Inteview in English, Jac Heijer with Ogden, 27 May 1982, Amsterdam.

Stanislavsky, Reinhardt, and Copeau—most have achieved something memorable.

The Werkteater actors needed two years to come to know and trust each other. Only with trust and a deep sense of responsibility for each other could they practice the mutual criticism so vital to their continued growth.

After this formative period—their youth, as it were—came four or five years in which they undertook major group projects, including *Twilight*, in which their own personal dynamics determined the dynamics of the theatrical event. *Twilight* was built on their struggle in their relationships with each other. They took their feelings about that struggle and focused them on the subject of aging, in all its profoundly personal ramifications for each of them. That is why the play can provide dramatic insight into the human condition for people of all ages. Also in this middle period they discovered two principles for their playmaking: they learned to focus on a central character or a central group, and they learned to persist in trying to find out what they wanted to show. As the log of *Twilight* amply demonstrates, all their improvisations came to be marked by that persistence, and by an equally strong drive to create tightly built dramatic forms.

Over the next five or six years they moved into another phase, marked by two-person and solo performances, such as Joop Admiraal's *You Are My Mother* (see Figs. 26 and 27), and by movie and television work, such as *In for Treatment* and the film version of *A Hot Summer Night* (see Fig. 32). Their only large-group projects were their summer tent comedies.

The Werkteater grew so popular that by the 1980s it was no longer reaching new theater audiences at home in Amsterdam, and its full houses there consisted of devotees who responded with enthusiasm to almost anything the actors put on. Moreover, after so many years of creating plays together, the actors were tending to repeat themselves when working with each other in the same modes. The Werkteater had become an institution, and its increasingly complex affairs demanded more and more management from outside the company. Clearly, on Långbacka's scale the Werkteater had moved away from its earlier position as an extreme art theater. Like the leaders in some of Långbacka's six art theaters, the Werkteater members had begun to see their future in different ways.

In the early 1980s, having climbed from anonymity to international fame, the Werkteater was still changing. A greater number of the actors took brief leaves of absence. Each year from the beginning, a senior student or two from a Dutch theater school had joined the Werkteater as an apprentice for part of each season (theater schools in Holland require such an internship of their students before graduation). In the 1980s many more newcomers were appearing as guests at the Werkteater. Then for the 1984–85 season Shireen Strooker formed a "Werkteater II" there with six young actors from a group of nine who were suddenly made full company members, not guests as heretofore. Most significantly, instead of working collectively to develop large new works, the actors in this period created one-person shows, established workshops, constructed performance projects that combined young people with original members, collaborated individually with other theater groups, and moved into television and filmmaking. In fact, for a time late in its history the Werkteater became a kind of headquarters for all sorts of projects with a considerable variety of people, from children's theater to cinema.

From the single Werkteater organism, 1970–85, many organisms have grown, and one of the results has been *teaching* in the broadest sense of the word. One finds the same pattern throughout cultural history: where the original life has been developed fully and carefully, other lives will grow from it. Stanislavsky and the Moscow Art Theater produced Vakhtangov, Meyerhold, Boleslavsky, Michael Chekhov, and indeed the whole tradition of realistic acting in the Western world. The teaching and practice of Jacques Copeau inspired Charles Dullin, Jean-Louis Barrault, the collaborations of Louis Jouvet with the playwright Jean Giraudoux, and Michel Saint-Denis's leadership in the Royal Shakespeare Company, the Old Vic School, the Canadian National Theatre Institute, and the Julliard School at Lincoln Center in New York.

In like manner today, two influences are beginning to spread from the Amsterdam Werkteater: a body of deep work in acting techniques that can enable the person of the actor to transcend technique; and a kind of playwriting in which actor and playwright collaborate intimately or become one and the same person. Through these influences theater people may find ways of bridging the gap between the performance and the drama that began to appear with the work of Artaud.

That gap will not be bridged, however, by theater people who ignore or misunderstand the very special characteristics of the Werkteater's process. Those who would follow the Werkteater model must confront many dangers.

First, the Werkteater process can become a poor substitute for acting skill. Actors can profit from the Werkteater techniques of deep work at two stages in their careers: first near the beginning, when the techniques can help them learn how to be comfortable on stage, how to find emotions that they can connect with those of their fellow players, and how to engage the attention of an audience; and then at maturity, when the techniques can encourage them to transcend technique and achieve genuine individual artistry. It is at this threshold of transcendence in the mature actor that the Werkteater model becomes most effective. Unfortunately, most actors simply do not know when in their careers they have reached that point. In mid-career an actor needs sustained training in the traditional skills of voice and speech and movement. During that period Werkteater methods can provide opportunities for on-the-spot coaching in traditional skills, but the skills must be there to work with. If pursued by immature or inept actors, these methods can quickly lead to sloppiness and self-indulgence.

Another danger of following the Werkteater model has to do with audience contact. When working to create a safe place in which to experiment, young actors can easily forget about the necessary discipline of playing to, and playing with, spectators. The Werkteater performers fought this tendency in themselves by regularly presenting open rehearsals followed by discussions with their audiences.

The style of playmaking, which is so important to this approach, poses its own risks. Actors who have developed a collective method of playmaking, and used it exclusively for a long period of time, find it difficult to take up written roles of any complexity. A great deal of extra effort must go into connecting the two modes; indeed it must be a conscious effort somewhat like learning how to translate from one language into another.

To give their corporate playmaking more than superficial impact, a group of actors must work together intimately for many months, if not for many years. But any intense working relationship is hard to sustain; at best, the actors can grow weary of each other's habits, like partners in a tired marriage; at worst, they can fight once too often and split up. And where the central creative impetus must continue to come from within one's self, instead of from the text of a great drama, an actor-playmaker can easily become stale and repetitive. When play and player are so intimately joined, the two can spiral together downward as well as upward.

An acute challenge lies in the acceptance and use of colleagues' criticism. The Werkteater actors could thrive on the discipline of regular self-criticism: mutual criticism of their presentations to each other, and collective and individual analysis of their public productions. This tradition was one of their most sustaining practices, and it supported their performances in ways that most audience members never saw. Yet for most artists who try to work closely together, this sort of criticism is the most difficult and potentially destructive practice imaginable.

Most actors, accustomed to working on an already written role, are simply not prepared to exercise the self-generating originality the Werkteater's processes require. Most do not have the special resilience of spirit needed to dig a role out of themselves, giving and receiving deep feelings in a painfully slow collective effort to achieve dramatic coherence. To try out the Werkteater processes for specific and limited purposes can be helpful at any level, but to sustain those processes for long periods demands a rare kind of person.

Finally, in the Werkteater model the language of the play is largely generated by the actors themselves. Traditional theater begins with what an individual playwright can contribute: ideally, a special richness of language, a coherence of theme, a complexity of inner and outer structure, and a large and pervasive idea. To duplicate this contribution collectively is a formidable challenge. When immature actors function as playwrights, their language seldom rises above the banal: what one usually hears is monosyllabic and dull, or a verbal smokescreen that hides an inner life instead of opening it out for the audience. Only the forceful leadership of the stimulator and the extremely careful attention that the actors would give to words, sentences, and verbal cadences enabled the Werkteater to produce dialogue that occasionally reached a poetic level. All of the Werkteater people care a great deal about language, and all of them have a definite gift for it. Furthermore, it is the stimulator who would work directly with the actors to create a coherence of themes and to lead them in the common search for a central vision, functions performed in the traditional theater by the playwright and the director. In many alternative theater groups the use of improvisational structures fails primarily because the actors have not gathered around a strong playwright-director figure. Even in the Werkteater, when the wrong company member assumed the role of stimulator, the project crashed.

Actors for the Theater of Tomorrow

If the future of great theater ultimately rests on the shoulders of powerful actors, a key question arises: what generates their power? In part the answer is *presence*—a rare gift that defies analysis but which the original Werkteater actors all possess. In part, however, the source of power is something more easily identified, and something that can be strengthened by hard work: deep and unshakable self-confidence. The original Werkteater actors are very different as individuals, and they have had their share of self-doubts and inner confusions, but deep down, all of them know that they exert real force on stage. This knowing is not entirely a product of thinking or becoming aware of oneself, however. Part of it is something instinctive, and that is probably what makes it compelling.

As Rense Royaards said, "No fear—just go out and play." That is what the Werkteater actors learned to do—by constantly developing new pieces, by playing under intimate conditions, and by facing a variety of different audiences. They learned, and gave depth to their plays, by opening themselves up and dealing with weaknesses rather than hiding them. And they learned from criticism by asking each other and their audiences, "Is this right?" When other troupes in the future look back to the Werkteater as a model, they will see this as one of their most significant achievements: they never stopped learning how to make use of constructive criticism.

When a Werkteater performance would get under way, it was spontaneous and contagious. Nowhere could one see this effect more strikingly than in the faces of children at a Werkteater production (Fig. 43). When the Werkteater actors did acrobatics, the children wanted to join in. The actors knew this and incorporated stunts with children from the audience into their own stunt-filled scenarios. Sometimes they would bring the children into the action immediately after a production (Fig. 44), but one could hardly tell where the production ended and the acrobatic epilogue began. This sort of performing is as infectious for adults as it is for children.

When looking to the Werkteater for signs that point toward new theater, one must begin by recalling the universal power of play. In a piece called *Hello Fellow*, in 1976, Rense Royaards began to develop the character of a street person called Chadowski, and eventually he was playing not only *for* an audience but *with* an audience. On 30 April 1980, Coronation Day in the Netherlands, and again on 21 November 1981, for a massive antinuclear demonstration, Rense went into the streets of Amsterdam as Chadowski (Fig. 45). He did this as a kind of personal demonstration, together with a couple of other Werkteater actors in their roles from *Hello Fellow*. Chadowski drinks too much, has strong political opinions, and is seldom logical but always very clear. "When you play a role in the street, you can enter into all

FIGURE 43. Shireen Strooker
and Herman Vinck, with technician Nico de Wit (left),
in *Quietly to Bed*, 1980.

The act of performance is contagious. Children
are invited on stage to play with the actors.

FIGURE 44. Actors, left to right: Gerard Thoolen,
Herman Vinck, Rense Royaards, and Frank Groothof.
After a performance of *Quite Normal*, 1977.

FIGURE 45.
No fear—just go out and play.
Rense Royaards as a bum in Amsterdam,
21 November 1981, during an antinuclear
demonstration. A role developed
since 1976 in the indoor
production of *Hello Fellow*.

the situations that you wish," says Rense. "As Chadowski I am free to use everything—all of my madness. I can shout and dance."[2] In Figure 45 he is helping an Amsterdam policeman with crowd control.

For tomorrow's theater, what the Werkteater points to above all is a return to the power of the actor. "What is theater and what is reality?" Rense asks. "Reality is only what you think you are in this world." What Rense is doing is not simply street theater. He is testing his powers as an actor, exorcising his fears, engaging in playmaking, and connecting constantly with participants in the event who are not actors. "People take you seriously, not like an actor," he says. Rense is free—free to go out and play—and that after all is what people come to the theater for: to be free to play, and to find freedom in the playing. Whether in a theater, in a tent, or on the street, Rense's attitude is contagious because it thrives on self-acceptance and joie de vivre. Like all of the Werkteater actors, he knows his power on stage. And with that power he can bring about a recognition, a revelation, and a new spirit in his audience.

2. Interview in English, Rense Royaards with Ogden, 2 June 1982, Amsterdam.

Epilogue

In this volume I have presented the Werkteater as it came into being and then grew into a powerful actors' theater from 1970 to 1985. Most of its original members have left the company rather recently. It is evident that today each one of them individually is adapting Werkteater techniques and attitudes to his or her new situation, whether working in film and television or as a free-lance actor collaborating with a new playwright or as a member of another theater company.

Marja's story shows how and why the Werkteater people began to move out into different arenas. She wanted to work in television exclusively. The troupe did not wish to devote itself only to TV, and so in 1982 she found it necessary to leave. She now has her own video company and has produced some dozen television pieces, employing many principles of the Werkteater.

For the 1984–85 season the Werkteater suddenly added nine members and split into two groups: one with eleven actors, the other with seven. Shireen took charge of six newcomers, developing pieces as "Werkteater II," in a sense starting all over again where the founders had begun back in 1970. But by 1986 only three of the original company members remained.

A great strength of the original Werkteater ensemble lay in its holding together as a kind of collective. Their formation was a freak accident. It could have happened only in Holland, a small country at a cultural crossroads with a vigorous inner sense of democratic process. It also could have happened only at that peculiar moment of social upheaval in the late 1960s and early 1970s. And I seriously doubt that at any other time would the

Dutch Ministry have come around to supporting such an under-
taking. At the start the enemy was outside: the social establishment, traditional theater, and their own poverty. The fight against
the enemy bound the company members together. They needed
each other in order to survive. The substance of their plays was
that very struggle, both personal and as a group. Then with time
the external enemy vanished, while the force of holding together remained. So that toward the end a company member,
like Marja, would have to leap out of the group in order "to work
in a new way"—the company's original goal. The group would
then close ranks.

In 1974 the company had added Olga and Frank; in 1980,
Frank's brother René. In the late 1970s the troupe had begun to
work in film and television. But they had never managed to find
satisfactory ways of collaborating over extended periods with
nonmembers. Their own history provided environment and raw
material for dramatic invention. The longer they remained together, the stronger their own history became and the more
difficult it was for an outsider to enter into their midst.

Today Olga as an actress is working with playwrights. So are
Cas and Rense. Cas is playing in a classical repertory as well.
Helmert is the artistic director of a theater in Arnhem, where he
fosters the creation of original works using Werkteater methods
in addition to staging traditional plays, often in radical interpretations. Individually Olga, Gerard, and Peter act almost constantly in films. Peter (who left the company in 1977) is also now
engaged in his fifth one-man show. Rense is a free-lance actor
and director, preparing to return to develop theater pieces in
Latin America. His book, *Who Do You Come From, God or the
Devil?* (1982), records his first such experience.[1] Hans manages a
theater in Amsterdam and develops new plays; at the moment
he is working with Shireen on a piece about AIDS. Shireen has
just finished evolving an original work with a young company that
she formed, and, steadily building on Werkteater techniques, she
is about to develop a project in connection with the founding of a

---

1. Rense Royaards, *Van wie komen jullie, van god of van de duivel?* (Utrecht: Van
Boekhoven-Bosch, 1982).

new national theater in Holland. Joop is touring his one-man show and will soon join a repertory company in Amsterdam as an actor. Frank and René continue to perform their two-man show while producing and acting in other plays as part of their own production company. There they also evolve pieces along Werkteater lines. At the Werkteater itself Yolande, Daria, and Herman are seeking to weld the newcomers into a genuine ensemble, to create plays with them, and to undertake very particular versions of traditional pieces, experimenting with a number of forms of collaboration.

Actors in the Company and Chronology of Works (by Season)

Actors in the Company

Joop Admiraal	(1972–85)
Yolande Bertsch	(1970–)
Cas Enklaar	(1970–85)
Peter Faber	(1970–77)
Frank Groothof	(1974–86)
René Groothof	(1980–86)
Marja Kok	(1970–84)
Jan Joris Lamers	(1970–71)
Hans Man in't Veld	(1970–85)*
Daria Mohr	(1970–)
Rense Royaards	(1970–84)
Shireen Strooker	(1970–86)
Gerard Thoolen	(1970–80)
Herman Vinck	(1970–)
Helmert Woudenberg	(1970–82)
Olga Zuiderhoek	(1974–82)

Werkteater company roster based on *Werkteater, teaterwerk sinds 1970*, ed. Rense Royaards (Utrecht: Van Boekhoven-Bosch, 1980) and *Brieven en foto's, Werkteater 1980–1985*, ed. Cas Enklaar (Rotterdam: Hard Werken, 1985).

* Half-time work for the Company during the 1985–86 season.

1984–1985 Season

WERKTEATER	WERKTEATER II
Joop Admiraal	Shireen Strooker
Yolande Bertsch	Toon Agterberg
Anne Buurma	Judith Hees
Cas Enklaar	Kenneth Herdigein
Frank Groothof	Neel Holst
René Groothof	Lieneke le Roux
Hans Man in't Veld	Maarten Wansink
Daria Mohr	
Paul Prenen	
Carla Reitsma	
Herman Vinck	

Werkteater Seasons, 1970–1986

1970–1971

1. *Dream Project (Dromenprojekt)*
Cast included Yolande, Cas, Marja, Jan Joris, Hans, Daria, and Gerard. About dreams. Never in a finished form. Multiple casting of the roles. Freely adapted text. Concluded with a performance, put together in a few days, of *Pelléas and Mélisande*, by Maurice Maeterlinck. November 1970–January 1971. Performed for the other half of the group on 29 January 1971.

2. *Truth Project (Waarheidsprojekt)*
Cast included Peter, Rense, Shireen, Herman, and Helmert. Power struggle for truth among five clowns. November 1970–March 1971. Five public performances in March 1971.

List of works for 1970–80 based on *Werkteater, teaterwerk sinds 1970*, ed. Rense Royaards (Utrecht: Van Boekhoven-Bosch, 1980), 155–66; for 1980–85, *Brieven en foto's, Werkteater 1980–1985*, ed. Cas Enklaar (Rotterdam: Hard Werken, 1985), 58–70; and for 1985–86, author's correspondence with the Werkteater.

The theater of the Werkteater, referred to in this chronology, is located at Spuistraat 2 (formerly 10 Kattengat Street), Amsterdam. It is a renovated factory in the heart of the city.

3. *Paradiso*
Series of short sketches without text (but with costumes, songs, dances), created at the request of Gert-Jan Dröge of the Paradiso Center and performed by the whole company.
  a. "Babies Murder Their Babysitter" ("Babies vermoorden hun oppas"), 20 November 1970 (and 27 May 1971, for "Artists Support North Vietnam," in Enschede).
  b. "Babies Murder Sint and Piet [St. Nicholas and Black Pete]" ("Babies vermoorden Sint en Piet"), 4 December 1970.
  c. "Babies and the Birth of Christ" ("Babies en de geboorte van Christus"), 18 December 1970.
  d. "Babies with Tambourines" ("Babies met de tamboerijnen"), 22 January 1971.
  e. "Jungle Sketch" ("Jungle-akt"), 5 February 1971.
  f. "The Boxing Ring" ("De bokskring"), 19 February 1971.
  g. "Colonial Liberation" ("Dekolonisatie"), 12 March 1971 (created for the Colonial Liberation Congress at the RAI Exhibition Hall and performed in the Paradiso Center).
  h. "Tea Time" ("De theevisite"), 25 March 1971 (and 22 May 1971 for "Artists Support North Vietnam," in Tilburg).
  i. "Little Nemo in Dreamland" ("Kleine Nemo in Dromenland"), 24 April 1971.
  j. "Little Nemo and the Harem" ("Kleine Nemo en de haremdames"), 21 May 1971.

4. *Lucifer*
The whole group worked on this piece by Joost van den Vondel, led by Jan Joris, Rense, and Shireen. The actors used the text as a starting point only, resulting in *To Conform or Not to Conform*. February 1971.

5. *To Conform or Not to Conform (Aangepast—Onaangepast)*
Improvisations on this theme. Two public performances by the whole group.

6. *Loneliness (Eenzaamheid)*
Improvisations on this theme by the whole group, derived from discussion of it by "Alternative Service" at St. James's Church, Haarlem, 25 April 1971.

7. *Games with Children (Spelen met kinderen)*
At the Montessori School in Amsterdam, with the whole

group. In the Theater Barn, Haarlem (founded by Hans, and Jan van Galen, 1969), with Peter, Marja, and Rense.

8. *Vietnam Evenings (Vietnam-Avonden)*
Sketches by Peter and Rense at Vietnam demonstrations.

9. *Allez-hop*
Commissioned by the Residence Orchestra with a piece of music, called "Allez-hop," by Luciano Berio, including two songs sung by Cathy Berberian. Conductor: M. Tabachnik. Clowns (the whole group) discover, take possession of, fight over, and wreck The Enormous Chair. Performance at the Congress Hall in The Hague, 15 May 1971.

10. *Summer on the Road (Zomer op straat)*
A little variety show, always changing, about twenty minutes in length. Performed on a tarp three or four times a day, with acrobatics, songs, jokes, fairy tales ("The Louse and the Flea," "Stupid Hans," "The Musicians of Bremen"), dramatized stories from the newspaper, and sung versions of weather reports.

11. *Workshop*
Given by the whole group with students at the adult school in Bergen. Each company member worked with an assigned group on an act of Shakespeare's *Richard III*. On the final evening the acts of the play were performed in order.

12. *The Evening Adventures of Beethoven (De avonduren van Beethoven)*
Performed by the whole group for NCRV television. Satirical illustrated story about art and artists. Concept: John Murat, Hugoké, and Rense Royaards. Music: Louis Andriessen. Director: Rense Royaards. Television broadcast September 1971.

1971–1972

1. *Small Projects (Kleine projekten)*, Autumn 1971
First series:
"Peggy Lee Dance" ("Peggy Lee dansje") and "Butterfly Sketch" ("Vlinderakt"; catching butterflies), with Yolande, Hans, and Herman.
"Animal Project" ("Dierenprojekt"; animal improvisations), with Peter, Daria, Rense, and Helmert. Performed once at the anniversary of the Academy for Expression, Utrecht.

"The Maids" ("De meiden"; improvisations based on *The Maids*, by Jean Genet), with Cas and Shireen. Stimulator: Marja. Performed once at the anniversary of the Academy for Expression.

Second series:

"Communications Project" ("Kommunikatie-projekt"), with Cas, Hans, Daria, and Rense.

"Chair-Table" ("Stoel-Tafel"; improvisations with two pieces of furniture), with Yolande and Peter.

"Tables" ("Tafels"; a piece with two men, each at a table), with Marja, Herman, and Helmert. Stimulator: Marja.

Third series:

"Chinese Li" (a story constructed by means of tarot cards), with Yolande, Hans, and Helmert.

"The Stair" ("De trap"; improvisations around a stepladder), with Cas, Peter, and Marja.

2. *Playing the Game of Goose (Ganzenborden)*

Cast included Yolande, Cas, Peter, Rense, and Herman. Stimulator: Herman. Players throw dice and move on the squares of a goose game drawn on the floor, where each numbered square contains an instruction. Played twice publicly at the Theater of the Werkteater. October–November 1972.

3. *The Birthday Party (Het verjaardagsfeest)*, by Harold Pinter

Cast included Marja, Hans, Daria, and Helmert. Stimulator: Shireen. Free adaptation of the play. Performed three times in the Theater of the Werkteater, December 1971, and once at the opening of the "Mokum Festival," at the Mickery Theater, Amsterdam, 30 March 1972.

4. *Temple Drake*

Project created by the whole group based on William Faulkner's novel *Sanctuary.* Developed under Marja's leadership 12–20 January 1972. All scenes performed one after the other (the actors in multiple roles) on 20 January 1972. Thereafter it was decided to stop this project and to begin with *In a Mess.*

5. *In a Mess (Toestanden;* sometimes called *Knots)*

Project created by the whole group, inspired by the work of Foudraine, Laing, and Fromm. Stimulator: Marja. About family and insanity and democratizing a psychiatric institution. (The first large, long-developed improvisatory work by the company. Subsequently performed in major medical institutions in Holland, as well as in the Theater of the Werkteater.) First public Evening Workshop 2 February 1972. Final performance 1 April 1975.

6. *Red Point (Rode stip)*
Improvisations by the whole group linked to an urban renewal demonstration in Haarlem, 18 February 1972.

7. *Games with Children (Spelen met kinderen)*
Young People's Theater Day, the Shaffy Theater, Amsterdam, 8 April 1972.

8. *Child and Environment (Kind en leefmilieu)*
Fairy tales and participatory games for children in the Bosco-tent at the Floriade Exhibition, Amsterdam, 22 June 1972.

9. *Joyce and Waldo*
Participation by the whole group in a film by Bram van Erkel, with and for children. Made by children at the Merkelbach School, Amsterdam, with company's assistance. Werkteater actors played parents and teachers. KRO television, broadcast 8 July 1972.

10. *Vietnam Demonstration (Vietnam-Demonstratie)*
Company sat on a wagon, writing and handing out funeral announcements, 29 April 1972.

11. *The Finals (De finale)*
Parody by the whole group of a television game show. Done for the Paradiso Center, Amsterdam, 22 April 1972. Also performed at the Vietnam demonstration in the Amsterdamse Bos (Park), 30 April 1972, and at the 1972 Olympic Games in the Spielstrasse (Olympic Games Street) in Munich.

12. *Allez-hop*
Repeat performances 15 June at the Royal Theater, in The Hague (Holland Festival); and 20 June in the Carré Theater, Amsterdam.

13. *To You*
Created by the whole group for the Holland Festival, with a poem by Adrian Mitchell and music by Peter Schat. It took place under a large, blue cloth lying in the central playing space of the Carré Theater, in the round: movements of bodies under

the cloth, sounds, and now and then heads appearing through holes in the cloth. Carré Theater, Amsterdam, 20 June 1972.

14. *Summer on the Road (Zomer op straat)*

About the same combination of acrobatics, news stories, songs, and fairy tales as in the previous year.

15. *Workshop*

Work on fairy tales. Adult school in Bergen, 29 July–6 August 1972.

16. *Spielstrasse*

A show for the Spielstrasse (Olympic Games Street) on the grounds of the Olympic Games in Munich, 25–31 August 1972.

   a. "All People Will Be Brothers" ("Alle Menschen werden Brüder"): a ballet of sports gestures during the singing of the German text.

   b. "Parable of the Sportsman" ("Parabel van de sportman"): a simple, visual sketch of the life of a top athlete.

   c. "The Finals" ("Das Finale"): German version.

The show was performed three or four times a day.

1972–1973

1. *Angola*

Short sketch created at the invitation of Amnesty International. Performed four times, September–December 1972.

2. *It's Only a Girl ('T is maar een meisje)*

Created by the whole group for NCRV television with director Gerard Rekers. Loose, cabaret-type scenes about women's liberation, influenced by Germaine Greer's *The Female Eunuch*. Thirteen performances, nine of them at the Theater of the Werkteater, September–October 1972. Television broadcast 13 February 1973.

3. *Employers' Council Project, KLM (Ondernemingsraad-projekt)*

Created by the whole group. Commissioned by KLM Airline for a series of study evenings aimed at better insight into and discussion of the functions of the Employers' Council. In simple, very visual scenes a sketch of the inception and growth of the company up to and including the establishment of the Employers' Councils Act. Discussion groups followed, in which the company took part in order to gather material for improvisations that were then presented to the entire gathering. Eleven study evenings in Noordwijkerhout, autumn 1972.

4. *Crime (Misdaad)*

Created by the whole group, in collaboration with Peter Hoefnagels. Stimulator: Helmert. About small, individual crime and large-scale (governmental? multinational?) crime. (The second large, long-developed improvisatory work by the company. Subsequently performed in major prisons in Holland, as well as in the Theater of the Werkteater.) First public Evening Workshop 28 March 1973. Final performance 14 April 1976.

5. *Election Project (Verkiezingsakt)*

Created at the request of the Workers' Party (Partij v.d. Arbeid) to get out the voters. Four street performances.

6. *Chile*

Street performance created at the request of the Evert Vermeer Foundation to focus attention on Allende's socialist experiment. Five performances.

7. *Holland and . . . (Nederland en . . .)*

Summer show, now on a stage with a tent covering. Slapstick, songs, the fairy tale "Zwaan kleef aan" ("White Swans/ Black Swans"), and *The Finals.*

8. *Oslo*

In conjunction with Dutch Week, performances in the street (various sketches), in the tent (the summer show), and in the Sonja Henie Center in Høvikodden (*In a Mess*). However, because *In a Mess*, which was half in English, did not seem to catch on, the company also performed the summer show in the Sonja Henie Center plus some sketches inspired by that space: for example, a song from *The Magic Flute* in the awards box of the Center, by Hans and Daria.

1973–1974

1. *Greet Gerritsen*

Commissioned by the Social Services Foundation of Middelburg. A social drama, twenty minutes in length. Four performances.

2. *Small Projects (Kleine projekten)*
   a. *Twilight (Avondrood)*
      Cast included Joop, Yolande, Marja, Daria, and Shireen.
      Stimulator: Shireen. Project begun without a theme or
      story. The theme that emerged was aging and death. Per-
      formed once in the Theater of the Werkteater.
   b. *Gang (Bende)*
      Cast included Frank Groothof (guest), Rense, Gerard, and
      Helmert. About fear and power struggle in a group.
   c. *Glasses and Braces (Brillen en beugels)*
      Cast included Peter, Hans, Herman. Stimulator: Peter.
      About children's fears. Performed nine times in different
      locations; performed for children during the summer tours
      of 1974 and 1975.

3. *Twilight (Avondrood)*
   The small project (2a) became a project by the whole group,
now focused more on the old people's home. About people who
are waiting for death. (The third large, long-developed improvisatory work by the company.) First public Evening Workshop 19
March 1974. Last performance 12 May 1977.

4. *Street Theater in Bonn (Straatteater Bonn)*
   For a street theater festival. A family of fat people taking a
stroll in Bonn. Prototype of *A Party for Nico*. 4, 5 May 1974.

5. *Circus Boem*
   Games with children from the town, in the tent, together
with a performance at the end of the week created with them.
(Part of the summer tour.) 11 July–24 August 1974.

6. *Office (Kantoor)*
   A sketch by Peter and Rense, performed at Nieuw Den-
nendal, a home for mental patients, on the evening before the
eviction of its patients and staff. 1 July 1974.

7. *Children's Play Mornings (Kinderspeelochtenden)*
   Led by Ria van der Woude at the Theater of the Werkteater. 3 November 1973–15 May 1974 (Saturday mornings).

8. *A Party for Nico (Het feest voor Nico)*
   Show for the tent (during the summer tour). Stimulator:
Rense. A fat family puts on a party to celebrate the graduation of
son Nico (who is thin) with a degree in engineering. Great con-

sternation when he announces his intention to help developing countries: Uncle Ben, who has paid for his education, does not like this at all. (The first major improvisatory work by the company for a summer tour.) First performance 22 May 1974. Final performance 25 September 1975. Performed during the summers of 1974 and 1975.

1974–1975

1. *Good Morning, Sir (Goedemorgen Meneer)*
Project created by all of the men in the group. Stimulator: Peter. An office—the dreams and desires of the people who work there. First performance 31 October 1974. Final performance 29 April 1975.

2. *Alex*
Project created by all of the women in the group. Stimulator: Yolande. Four sisters, a widow, and a dead man. First performance 21 November 1974. Final performance 14 February 1975.

3. *The Cabinet of Dr. Menotti (Het kabinet van Dr. Menotti)*
Created by the whole group in a few days as a Christmas surprise. Horror stories in a wax museum, designed for various spaces in the Theater of the Werkteater. Scenario: Helmert. Design and costumes: Cas. Eight performances.

4. *Men-and-Women Project (Man-Vrouwprojekt)*
Unrehearsed improvisations on this theme. Spring 1975. Four performances.

5. *A Party for Nico (La Fête pour Nico)*—French version
Performed at the Festival Mondial du Théâtre, Nancy, 15–19 May 1975.

1975–1976

1. *Nobody Home (Niet thuis)*
Project by Peter, Judith Hees (guest), Hans, and Shireen. About children in orphanages. First public Evening Workshop 28 October 1975. Final performance 17 October 1977.

2. *Aladin (Aladdin)*
Project by Frank, Gerard, Helmert, and Olga. Stimulator:

Helmert. Adaptation of the fairy tale. First public Evening Workshop 2 December 1975. Final performance 6 May 1977.

3. *Monsters*

Project by Joop, Yolande, Cas, Marja, Daria, Rense, and Herman. Stimulator: Marja. About "monsters" in the Barnum and Bailey Circus—"human oddities." The project came to an impasse. Film sequences about fat people were shot; from these developed *Thick Friends.*

4. *Thick Friends (Dikke vrienden)*

Fat people gather to protest discrimination against fat people. Later the setting became fat people in group therapy. The scenario was always very much improvised; only the characters were agreed upon beforehand.

5. *Quite Normal (Doodgewoon)*

Project by Yolande, Peter, Frank, and Gerard. Stimulator: Peter. Children's play for the summer tour, based on *The Lionheart Brothers*, by Astrid Lindgren. About the fear of death and overcoming the fear. Performed with various casts during the summers of 1976 and 1977.

6. *Hello Fellow! (Hallo medemens!)*

Piece created by the whole group for the tent (on the summer tour). Three society ladies try to establish contact with some street people and other fringe characters. (The second major improvisatory work by the company for a summer tour.) Performed during the summers of 1976 and 1977.

7. *In a Mess (Toestanden)*—Film version

Film director: Thijs Chanowski. Camera: Mat van Hensbergen. September 1975.

8. *Twilight (Abendrot)*—German version, for stage and television

Performed in Hamburg in the Malersaal, May 1975. German television broadcast 15 May 1975.

9. *Alcohol and Drugs*

Yolande, Marja, and Shireen work with people from the Center for Alcoholism and Drug Abuse.

10. *Office (Kantoor)*

Project by Peter and Rense for the Medical Committee, Vietnam.

1976–1977

1. *Scared to Death (Als de dood)*

Project by Yolande, Cas, Hans, Shireen, Gerard, Herman, Ivan Wolffers (a doctor), and Olga. Stimulator: Shireen. Loosely connected scenes about dying in a hospital. Performed in major Dutch hospitals as well as in the Theater of the Werkteater and other Dutch theaters. First public Evening Workshop, with *You've Got to Live with It* (together called *Dying [Sterven]*), 18 February 1977. Final performance 28 September 1979, at the Belgrade International Theater Festival (BITEF), Yugoslavia. (Members of the company divided into two groups. One developed *Scared to Death;* the other, *You've Got to Live with It.* What can be called the fourth large, long-developed improvisatory work by the company resulted in a pair of pieces, separate in performance but linked in theme. First public performances 11 March 1977: *Scared to Death,* in Utrecht, and *You've Got to Live with It,* in the Theater of the Werkteater. Later they were joined for the film *In for Treatment [Opname].*)

2. *You've Got to Live with It (Je moet er mee leven)*

Project by Joop, Peter, Frank, Marja, Daria, Rense, and Helmert. Stimulator: Marja. A story about dying in a hospital. Performed in major Dutch hospitals as well as in the Theater of the Werkteater and other Dutch theaters. First public Evening Workshop 18 February 1977. Final performance 28 September 1979, at the Belgrade International Theater Festival (BITEF), Yugoslavia.

3. *Camping*—A film

Created by the whole group. Film director: Thijs Chanowski. Scenario: Marja, Rense, and Helmert. Camera: Frans Bromet. An ironic look at Dutch society while camping.

1977–1978

1. *Marja and Shireen in the Kattengat Scene (Mar en Sien op Kattengat 10)*

Project by Marja and Shireen, begun as a "concert" (a personal, improvised presentation for the other company members), then performed publicly. The story of a lifelong friendship between two women. First public performance 19 January 1978. (In 1980 called *De Mar en Sien show.*)

2. *Cas and Joop (Cas en Joop)*

Project by Cas and Joop parallel to *Marja and Shireen.* The story of a friendship. First public performance 4 February 1978. Final performance 7 December 1979.

3. *Scared to Death, You've Got to Live with It, Mary and Syl* (*Mar en Sien,* only on 5 March)—English versions

Performed at the Oval House Theater and the Institute of Contemporary Arts, London, 28 February–5 March 1978.

4. *A Hot Summer Night (Een zwoele zomeravond)*

Created by the whole group for the tent (on summer tour). Idea: Marja. A Dutch provincial variety show with backstage catastrophes. Performed during the summers of 1978 and 1979, in the center ring of the new tent, with "The Cream Puffs" orchestra. (The third major improvisatory work by the company for a summer tour.)

5. *Buddies (Gabbers)*

Children's show for the summer tour. Idea: Shireen, Herman, and Helmert. Performed by Joop, Cas, Frank, and Gerard; then with various casts during the summer of 1978. Two men from the electric company interrupt a children's show and then put on a piece themselves.

1978–1979

1. *Sticking on Labels (Etiketten plakken)*

Project by Rense, Helmert, Olga, and Frits Lambrechts (guest). About the results of unemployment on daily life. First performance 28 February 1979.

2. *Who's Afraid of Virginia Woolf? (Wie is bang voor Virginia Woolf?),* by Edward Albee

A very short version of Edward Albee's play, fairly true to the text, performed by Joop, Cas, Hans, and Gerard at the Theater of the Werkteater. Four performances, December 1978.

3. *One of Them (Zus of zo)*

Project about homosexuality by Joop, Cas, Hans, and Gerard. First performance 13 February 1979.

4. *Scared to Death (Wie der Tod)*—German version
Performed in Hamburg for Théâtre des Nations, 10–13 May 1979.

5. *Neutron Bomb (Neutronen bom)*
Protest sketch. Two performances on the Dam Square, Amsterdam.

6. *Quietly to Bed (Welterusten)*
Children's play for the summer tour, created with the assistance of Peter Faber: Frank, Hans, Daria, Rense, and Olga. About fears in the night. First performance 24 May 1979.

7. *Frank and René (Frank en René)*
Improvisations by Frank and his brother (as a guest), René Groothof, for children in hospitals.

8. *In for Treatment (Opname)*—A film
Created by the whole group. Direction: Marja, and Erik van Zuylen. Camera: Robbie Müller. Based on *Scared to Death* and *You've Got to Live with It*. Premiere 19 October 1979.

9. *Hello Fellow! (Hallo medemens!)*—Television version
Television director: Egbert van Hees. Adaptation: Rense and Shireen. Filmed March 1979. Broadcast by VARA television 4 January 1980.

1979–1980

1. *Uncle Vanya (Oom Wanja)*, by Anton Chekhov
Performed by Joop, Cas, Frank, René Groothof (guest), Hans, Daria, Shireen, and Herman. The Chekhov text with minor cuts. Translation: Chiem van Houweningen and Ton Lutz. Direction (*Regie*): Shireen. Technical work: Henk Veltkamp. (Note: from here on the word *stimulator* does not appear in the chronology of seasons as published by the Werkteater.) 2 November–15 December 1979.

2. *Twilight (Abendrot)*—Special television version in German
Performed by Joop, Cas, Marja, Hans, Daria, Rense, Shireen, Gerard, Herman, Helmert, Olga, and Devika Strooker (guest). Adaptation: Shireen and Rense. Camera: Klaus Brix. Producer: Dagmar Voss. Filmed in Hamburg by the Norddeutscher Rundfunk, January 1980. Television director: Jochen Wolf, with Shireen.

3. *Very Special (Gewoon weg)*

Project sponsored by the Commission for Special Education about children in special education schools. Created by Daria and Marja. Performed by Frank, Marja, Daria, Herman, and guests René Groothof, Rob Boonzajer, and Dorijn Curvers. 20 January 1980–24 March 1981.

4. *Waldeslust (Bosch en lucht;* although literally meaning "woods and air," the title is translated by the Werkteater—and in the present book—as *Waldeslust)*

Project created by the whole group for the summer tour with the tent, with guests (at various times) Dorijn Curvers, Arjan Ederveen, René Groothof, Kees Prins, Rob Boonzajer, Roel van Eekhout, Ida Mager, and Maria van der Woude. Direction: Marja and Shireen. Music: Paul Prenen. Technical work: Henk Veltkamp, Charles Kersten, and Frank van der Steen. Based partly on *Very Special* and partly on a new idea about Dutch tourists. (The fourth major improvisatory work by the company for a summer tour.) First performance 15 May 1980.

5. *Long Live the Queen (Leve de koningin)*

Street performances by René Groothof and Rense as Piet Smit and Chadowski (their roles in *Hello Fellow!*) during the coronation of Queen Beatrix, 30 April 1980.

6. *Maria e Laura (De Mar en Sien show)*—Italian version

Performed by Marja, Shireen, Frank, and Roel van Eekhout (guest). Translation: Bertie van Pinxteren. Technical work: Henk Veltkamp. International Theater Festival, Florence, 10 and 11 May 1980.

7. *Quietly to Bed*

Children's play for the summer tour, second season in repertory, created under the direction of Peter Faber: Cas, Frank, Marja, Hans, Daria, Rense, Shireen, and Herman, with guests René Groothof, Rob Boonzajer, and Paul Prenen (music). 25 May 1979–5 July 1980.

8. *Dutchman,* by Leroi Jones

Amsterdam Theater School project by apprentices Ada Bouwman and Glenn Durfort. Translation: Cees Nooteboom. Supervision: Hans, Helmert, and Bambi Uden. Summer performances in a bus beside the tent, 23 May–5 July 1980.

1980–1981

1. *Defense and Resistance (Verweer en verweer)*
Amsterdam Theater School project by apprentices Ada
Bouwman and Glenn Durfort. Supervision: Hans and Helmert.
5 September–22 November 1980.

2. *Uncle Vanya*
With cast changes, including additions of Helmert and Arjan Ederveen (guest). 19 January–8 April 1981.

3. *Marja and Shireen*
Marja and Shireen, with either Joop, Frank, or Kees Prins
(guest) and other guests. 19 January 1978–8 April 1981.

4. *Waldeslust*
In the Carré Theater, Amsterdam, 14–18 November 1980.

5. *Ristorante Guatelli*
Italian family drama with music. Created by René (now a
regular company member), Frank, Hans, Herman, and guests
Dorijn Curvers, Kees Prins, Arjan Ederveen, Rob Boonzajer,
and Paul Prenen (also music). 12 December 1980–17 April 1981.

6. *The Caretaker (De huisbewaarder)*, by Harold Pinter
Performed by Frank, René, and Helmert. Translation: G. K.
van't Reve. Director: Helmert. Technical work: Charles Kersten.
6 February–1 May 1981.

7. *Clothes (Kleren)*
Cas, with guests Dorijn Curvers, Arjan Ederveen, and
Kees Prins. 30 April–15 May 1981.

8. *Incidental Project—Institute for Psychology and Pedagogy*
Performed by Joop, Frank, Hans, Shireen, Herman, and
guests Rob Boonzajer, Dorijn Curvers, Arjan Ederveen, Die-
derik Lohman, Kees Prins, and Devika Strooker. Meervaart,
Amsterdam, 30 March 1981.

9. *On the Other Hand (Niettegenstaande)*
Performed by Yolande and Olga, with apprentices Ernst
Boreel or Peter Lunow. Influenced by a training period with
Saskia Noordhoek Hegt (January 1981). Technical work: Henk
Veltkamp. A project about two women and their relationship
with a man. 13 April 1981–3 April 1982.

10. *Improvisational Project—Prior to Elections*
Performed by René and Rense. Museumplein, Amsterdam, 23 May 1981.

11. *Waldeslust*—German version of *Bosch en lucht*
Translation: Peter Schreiber. First performance 2 June 1981 in Stuttgart. Then Berlin, Cologne, Hamburg. Final performance 4 July 1981 in Zurich. German television record of Cologne performance: complete broadcast, 19 July 1981; partial broadcast, "Theater der Welt," R. W. Fassbinder, 11 November 1981.

12. *One of Them (Zus of zo)*—English version
Cas and Joop, with guests Arjan Ederveen and Kees Prins. Later version with Cas, Joop, and Hans. Translation: Martin Cleaver. Technical work: Charles Kersten. First performances 11–16 August 1981, ICA, London. Then Los Angeles (Fountain Theater) and New York (Warren Robertson Theater). Final performance 17 January 1982 in New York.

Also during the 1980–81 season:

Olga performed in a production by Bram Vermeulen, *The Future Will Really Happen (De toekomst gaat het helemaal maken)*. Helmert performed in *Mayakovsky* at the Onafhankelijk Toneel, Toneelschuur (Independent Theater, Theater Barn), Haarlem. Rense worked on a project in Mexico under the auspices of the University of Vera Cruz.

1981–1982

1. *A Hot Summer Night (Een zwoele zomeravond)*—A film
Created by the whole group. Directors: Frans Weisz and Shireen. Scenario: Marja. Camera: Robbie Müller. Music: "The Cream Puffs." Production Coordinator: Hans. Executive Producer: Frits Harkema. Based on theater piece with the same title. Filmed September–October 1981. Premiere 10 March 1982.

2. *The Rules of the House (De regels van het huis)*
Performed by Daria, Herman, and guests Pierre Bokma, Ada Bouwman (or Yolande), and Arie Kant. After 1 February, Pierre, Ada, and Arie replaced respectively by René, Dorijn Curvers (guest), and Hans. Based on an idea by Yolande, and Marijke Zwaan (guest, dramaturg). Design: Erik den Hartog.

Technical work: Mendel Frank. Society as represented by a family confronted with someone who is unfamiliar with our way of life. 3 November 1981–1 April 1982.

3. *Incidental Project—Demonstration Against Nuclear Weapons*

During the demonstration: Frank, René, and Rense. Evening, Paradiso Center: Yolande with guests Pierre Bokma, Ada Bouwman, and Arie Kant. 21 November 1981.

4. *Waldeslust*

Tour of Dutch theaters. 9 October–24 December 1981.

5. *Improvisational Evenings (Improvisatie avonden)*

Short scenes thought up from directives given on the spot. Olga, Marja, and guest Nico Bunink (piano). Later without Marja and with Helmert and guest Peter Faber (who had left the Werkteater officially in fall 1977). 24 November 1981–30 March 1982.

6. *You Are My Mother (U bent mijn moeder)*

Joop's solo project. About his visits with his mother. Joop plays himself as well as his mother. Direction: Jan Ritsema (guest). Technical work: Charles Kersten. First performance 1 December 1981. Joop was awarded the Louis d'Or for the performance.

7. *One of Them*

Performed by Joop, Cas, and Hans. Technical work: Olga. After American tour, at Kleine Komedie, Amsterdam, 25–30 January 1982.

8. *Improvisational Evenings*

Performed by Helmert and Olga, with guests Peter Faber and Nico Bunink (piano). 1–24 February 1982.

9. *Doctor Tom (Doktor Tom)*

Helmert's solo project. Based on images from Hopi Indian myths. Technical work: Henk Veltkamp. 2 February–8 May 1982.

10. *Incidental Project—Support for Argentinian Mothers*

Shireen, and Peter Faber (guest). About censorship in Argentina. Nieuwe Kerk, Amsterdam, March 1982.

11. *Waldeslust*

Carré Theater, Amsterdam, 2–10 March 1982.

12. *Traviata/Singing in the Rain*

Solos intertwined by Frank (*Traviata*) and Cas (*Singing in the Rain).* Music: Taco Kooistra, Huub Matthijsen, and Paul Prenen. 26 March 1982, 2 April 1982; also at Amsterdam Theater School, 2 April 1982.

13. *Ristorante Guatelli*
Summer tent version of the musical piece with the same title. The same players as before, without Kees Prins and with the addition of Joop and guests Roel van Eekhout and Kenneth Herdigein. Decor: Herman and Joop. Technical work: Henk Veltkamp and Charles Kersten. Supervision: Helmert. 22 May–18 September 1982.

14. *Incidental Project—Support for Amnesty International*
Performed by Shireen, Rense, and Peter Faber (guest). Carré Theater, Amsterdam, May 1982.

15. *The Gardens of Dorr (De tuinen van Dorr)*
Summer tent project—a fairy tale for children, based on the book with the same title by Paul Biegel. Performed by Hans, Daria, René, and guests Dorijn Curvers, Arjan Ederveen, Carla Reitsma, Kees Prins, Kenneth Herdigein, Paul Prenen (music), Rob Boonzajer, and Devika Strooker. Direction: Shireen. Decor: Ronald Timmerman and Paul Höhne. Technical work: Roel Velthorst and Claudio Guatelli. 26 May–7 November 1982.

16. *Incidental Project—International Building Center, Rotterdam*
Performed by Hans, with guests Peter Faber, Nico Bunink, Arjan Ederveen, Kees Prins, and Carla Reitsma. 3 June 1982.

17. *Evening Piece Two (Avondstuk II)*
A special work for the summer tent tour. Cast included Cas, Marja, Rense, Daria, Yolande, and guest Martine Nijhof. Technical work: Onno van der Wal, Charles Kersten, Henk Veltkamp, and Claudio Guatelli. (Instead of creating a fifth major improvisatory work for the summer tour of 1982, the company divided in half and created a pair of plays: *Evening Piece Two* and *Ristorante Guatelli.*) 24 June–25 September 1982.

18. *Incidental Project—Support for Argentinian Mothers*
Performed by Shireen with guests Glenn Durfort, Kenneth Herdigein, Ruurt de Maerschalck, Numa Moraez, Astrid Seriese, and Devika Strooker. Amazon Foundation, Amsterdam, September 1982.

Also during the 1981–82 season:

Cas and Marja performed in *From Afar (Aus der Fremde)*, by Ernst Jandl, at the Onafhankelijk Toneel (Independent Theater).

1982–1983

1. *Incidental Project—Medical Congress of General Practitioners*
Performed by Yolande, Hans, Daria, and Shireen, with guests Peter Lunow and Maarten Wansink. Odeon, Amsterdam, 5 November 1982.

2. *An Evening with Joan (Een avond met Joan)*
Cas's solo project, about Joan Crawford. Based on *Conversations with Joan Crawford*, by Roy Newquist, and *My Way of Life*, by Joan Crawford. Advisers: Marja and Joop. Technical work: Henk Veltkamp and Charles Kersten. 3 December 1982–3 March 1984.

3. *Incidental Project—Bankruptcy Congress, Junior Bar Association*
Performed by Hans, Herman, with guests Peter Faber, Geertrui Daem, Arjan Ederveen, and Kees Prins. Rhenen, 19 November 1982.

4. *The Owl and the Pussycat (Een blijspel?)*, by Bill Manhoff
Adapted and performed by Shireen and Hans. Adviser: Gerardjan Rijnders. Technical work: Lody Crabbendam. 7 December–21 December 1982.

5. *The Iron Road (De ijzeren weg)*
Herman's solo project, about his upbringing in Aalst, Belgium. Created in collaboration with Loek van Kesteren. Performed by Herman, with guests Geertrui Daem and Rob Boonzajer (also music). Decor: Herman, and Henk Veltkamp. Technical work: Henk Veltkamp. 16 December 1982–31 March 1983.

6. *Amor*
Performed by Marja with guests Charles Kersten, Robert Ouwerkerk, and Onno van der Wal. Combination of stage and video production. Closed performance, Theater of the Werkteater, 19 December 1982.

7. *Brood (Gebroed)*
Project by Frank and René, about their relationship as

brothers, past and present. Performed by Frank, René, and guest Paul Prenen (music). Supervision: guest Michiel Berkel. Technical work: Bas Steenstra. 7 January 1983–28 December 1984. (Continued independently from the Werkteater, 1986–87.)

8. *Seagull (Meeuw)*, by Anton Chekhov

Performed by Joop, René, Marja, Daria, with Ida Mager (administrative assistant of the Werkteater), and guests Krijn ter Braak, Peer Mascini, Ben van Doorn, Evert van der Meulen, Frans Weisz, and Olga Zuiderhoek (who had left the Werkteater after the 1981–82 season). In a later version Cas and Herman replaced Joop and Frans Weisz. Translation: Charles B. Timmer. Direction and design: Cas. Technical work: Charles Kersten, Henk Veltkamp, and Onno van der Wal. Assistance: Ron Termaat. 15 February 1983–7 May 1983; at the Teatro Festival, Parma, 23 and 24 April 1983.

9. *Incidental Project "A Gesture" (Ad hoc optreden "Een gebaar")*

Performed by Joop, Yolande, Cas, René, Hans, Daria, and Herman, with guests Esther Apituley, Hester Bolt, Boris Boonzajer, Rob Boonzajer, Glenn Durfort, Roel van Eekhout, Jessica Felsenthal, Joshua Felsenthal, Marie Groothof, Kenneth Herdigein, Charles Kersten, Marije Kweekel, Ida Mager, Martine Nijhof, Alissa van Slooten, Cari van Slooten, Gooike van Slooten, Devika Strooker, Henk Veltkamp, Erwin Vinck, Lotje Vinck, and Maria van der Woude. Carré Theater, Amsterdam, 16 and 17 May 1983.

10. *You Are My Mother (Du bist meine Mutter)*—German version of *U bent mijn moeder*

Translation: Monika Thé. Bremen, Bochum, Berlin, and Hamburg, 1 May–17 September 1983.

11. *You Are My Mother (Du bist meine Mutter)*—German and Dutch television versions

Filmed in Hamburg by the Norddeutscher Rundfunk. Director: Horst Königstein. Camera: Klaus Brix. Producer: Dagmar Voss. German premiere 5 December 1983; Dutch premieres 13 February 1984 (Theater of the Werkteater) and 30 August 1984 (public cinemas).

12. *Seagull (Meeuw)*—Television version

A fifty-minute version filmed in the Frisian Islands—Engelsmanplaat and Dalfsen. Performed by Joop, René, Shireen, Daria, Cas, and Herman, with Ida Mager (administrative assistant of the Werkteater), and guests Krijn ter Braak, Evert van der Meulen, and Olga Zuiderhoek. Adapter and director: Marja. Camera: Onno van der Wal. Sound: Charles Kersten and Henk Veltkamp. Producer: Rense. Filmed August 1983. Dutch premiere 20 February 1984.

Also during the 1982–83 season:

Frank worked on the opera *Ballast*, by Rob Hauser, produced by the Orkater Foundation. Shireen served as stimulator for two performance projects with students at the University of California, Berkeley: *Neglect* and *Ondine*.

NOTE: During the summer of 1983 there was no summer tent show.

1983–1984

1. *Fat Fingers (Dikke vingers)*, based on the play by Paul Haenen
    Performed by Shireen and Hans. Adviser: Gerardjan Rijnders. Technical work: Henk Veltkamp. On 30 March 1984, Hans replaced by Ischa Meijer (guest). 17 September 1983–25 April 1984.

2. *As It Is (Zoals het is)*—Video film
    Yolande and guests Dan Blokker, Karsten Blokker, Jacob Blokker, and Bodil Blokker-Veggerby. Concept: Yolande and guest Joke Menssink. In collaboration with Meatball and the NOS (Dutch television). Premiere broadcast 18 January 1984.

3. *Patience Please (Geduld a.u.b.)*
    Performed by René and Hans, with guests Jean Couprie, Gerard Draaisma, Sabine Eijsenring, Gert-Jan de Kleer, Leontien Koenders, Lineke Posthuma, Scaije Schuurmans, Roger Tiesema, and Hanny de Vrije. Created in conjunction with the Dutch Department for the Hearing Impaired and the Visual Theater Foundation. Theater of the Werkteater, 12 April and 19 October 1983, 25 February 1984. National Hearing Impaired Congress at Emmen, 20 October 1983.

4. *A Look at the Deaf World (Een blik op de dovenwereld)*—Nine video films

Performed by Daria, with Ruud Janssen from the Dutch Department for the Hearing Impaired. Premiere broadcast 20 October 1983.

5. *Dance of Death (Dodendans)*, based on the play by August Strindberg
Performed by Cas, René, and Shireen. Direction: Marja. Camera: Onno van der Wal. Sound: Charles Kersten. Combination of stage and video production. Closed performance at the Theater of the Werkteater, 29 January 1984.

6. *Good-bye (Adio)*
Performed by Joop, Yolande, Frank, and guest Paul Prenen (piano). Direction: Jan Ritsema. 31 January–21 December 1984.

7. *Incidental Project—Association of Police Officials*
Performed by Yolande and Hans, with guests Peter Faber, Toon Agterberg, Glenn Durfort, and Kenneth Herdigein. Congress of Police Officials at Hoogeveen, 11 May 1984.

8. *Dance of Death (Dodendans)*, based on the play by August Strindberg—Video film
Performed by Cas, René, and guests Els Ingeborg Smits, Koby de Klerq, Cumee Strooker. Direction: Marja. Camera: Onno van der Wal. Sound: Charles Kersten. Continuity: Bas Steenstra. General assistance: Thijs Bayens. Production coordinator: Anita van Reede. Filmed April 1984. Premiere broadcast SALTO (Amsterdam television), 31 August 1984.

9. *Between Heaven and Earth (Tussen hemel en aarde)*
Work for the summer tent tour. Performed by Joop, Hans, Daria, Shireen, and guests Toon Agterberg, Mouna Goeman Borgesius, Kenneth Herdigein, Jaap Jan de Kat Angelino, Joan Nederlof, and Bram Vermeulen and Edward B. Wahr (instrumental and vocal music). Direction: Shireen. Design: Jago Bo. Costumes: Maria van der Woude. Technical work: Henk Veltkamp, Leo van den Boogaard, Marc van Gelder, Hans Looye, and Pieter Rienks. 26 May–8 September 1984.

10. *Little Brothers (Broertjes)*
Children's play for the summer tent tour, based on *Brood*. Performed by Frank and René, with guests Peter de Jager, Paul Prenen (music). Technical work: Bas Steenstra. 26 May–26 December 1984. (Continued independently from the Werkteater, 1986–87.)

11. *Leichner Nr. 5* [a brand of stage makeup]
Work for the summer tent tour. Performed by Herman, with guests Rob Boonzajer, Karstine Hovingh, Martine Nijhoff, and Paul Prenen. Direction: Rense. Technical work: Claudio Guatelli, Jeroen Janssen. 16 June–1 September 1984.

12. *Creditors I* (*Schuldeisers I*)—Video film, working title
Performed by Marja, Joop, Rense, with Frans Weisz, Charles Kersten, and Onno van der Wal. May 1984.

13. *Creditors II*, based on the play by August Strindberg—Video film, working title
Performed by Cas, Marja, and Rense. Direction: Marja. Camera: Onno van der Wal. Light and sound: Charles Kersten. Continuity: Maria Juana Hughes. General assistance: Thijs Bayens. June 1984.

Also during the 1983–84 season:

Cas worked on the film *A Day at the Beach* (*Een dagje naar het strand*), by Theo van Gogh, and, in Hamburg, on the Norddeutscher Rundfunk television film *Rendezvous at Infinity* (*Treffpunkt im Unendlichen*), by Horst Königstein.

1984–1985

The 1984–85 season marked a radical change in the Werkteater with the formation of two groups: "Werkteater" and "Werkteater II." For the personnel roster of each, see the beginning of Appendix A.

1. *Ulrike*
Coproduction with the Amsterdam Theater School. Performed by Yolande, Daria, and Herman, with Tamar Baruch, Arend Bulder, Mieke Heesen, and Froukje van Houten. Direction: Jetty van der Meer. Script: Sophie Kassies. Design and sound: Louise Oeben, Matthijs Groené, Martin Cleaver. Lighting: Sophia France. Production coordinator: Liesbeth Smeenk. 19 September–27 October 1984.

2. *Incidental Project—Patients' Congress, Heart Foundation of Holland*
Performed by Toon Agterberg, Judith Hees, Neel Holst, Lieneke le Roux, and Maarten Wansink. Direction: Shireen.

Three performances at RAI Hall, Amsterdam, 20 October 1984. Closed performances at the Theater of the Werkteater, 6 and 7 November 1984. University Hospital, Leiden, 9 January 1985.

3. *Incidental Project*—*"Get Out of My Life" ("Blijf van m'n lijf") Foundation*
Performed by Kenneth Herdigein and Maarten Wansink. Created by Shireen. About battered women and the police. Paradiso Center, Amsterdam, 26 October 1984.

4. *Jungle Drums*
Performed by Cas, René, Anne Buurma, and Carla Reitsma. With passages from *Two Serious Ladies*, by Jane Bowles. 2 November–21 December 1984.

5. *Brood (Gebroed)*—Video film
Performed by Frank, René, and Paul Prenen. Direction: Jop Pannekoek. Videotaping 11 November 1984. Premiere broadcast 28 January 1987.

6. *Incidental Project*—*Educational TV, Adult Education*—Video film
Theme: "Women in the Minority." Performed by Shireen, Toon Agterberg, Judith Hees, Kenneth Herdigein, Neel Holst, Lieneke le Roux, and Maarten Wansink. Videotaping 8 January 1985. Premiere broadcast 3 February 1985.

7. *Romeo and Jeanette*, by Jean Anouilh
Performed by Shireen, Toon Agterberg, Judith Hees, Kenneth Herdigein, Lieneke le Roux, and Maarten Wansink. Direction: Shireen. Design: Jago Bo. Music: Bram Vermeulen. Costumes: Maria van der Woude. Technical work: Hans Westendorp. 2 February–1 November 1985.

8. *The Coronation of Poppea*, by Claudio Monteverdi (Libretto: Busenello)
A special version. Performed by Joop, Yolande, Frank, René, Daria, Herman, and Carla Reitsma. Direction: Jan Ritsema. Musical direction: Paul Prenen. Flute: Judith van den Bos. Cello: Tobias Prenen. 13 February–22 November 1985.

9. *Visit with Joan (Besuch bei Joan)*—German television adaptation of *An Evening with Joan*
Performed by Cas, with Trude Possehl. Adaptation and direction: Horst Königstein. Translation: Monika Thé. Camera:

Klaus Brix. Decor: Andreas Heller. Norddeutscher Rundfunk taping April 1985. Premiere (German) broadcast 14 October 1985.

10. *Somberman's Action (Somberman's aktie)*
Performed by Hans, Toon Agterberg, Judith Hees, Kenneth Herdigein, Lieneke le Roux, Maarten Wansink, and Johan Vigeveno (the Writer), and children of the Elleboog Children's Theater. Based on the novel *Somberman's aktie* by Remco Campert. Created for the opening ball of the National Book Week. Direction: Shireen. Music: Bram Vermeulen. Design: Jago Bo. Carré Theater, Amsterdam, 19–23 March 1985.

11. *Good-bye (Adio)*—German version
Performed by Joop, Yolande, Frank, and Paul Prenen (piano). Direction: Jan Ritsema. 10 April–29 September 1985.

12. *The Ugly Duckling (Het lelijke jonge eendje)*
Performance for children, in a summer festival tent. With Frank, René, Rob Groothof (guest), and Carla Reitsma. Music: Paul Prenen. Costumes: Maria van der Woude and Ankie Groothof. Design, painting: Joop. Based on the fairy tale by Hans Christian Andersen. 25 May–15 September 1985.

13. *Who Is Doing Somberman? (Wie doet Somberman?)*
Performed by Hans, Shireen, Willem Wagter or Herman, Toon Agterberg, Rob Duyker, Judith Hees, Kenneth Herdigein, Lieneke le Roux, Bram Vermeulen, Edward B. Wahr, and Maarten Wansink. Direction: Shireen. Assistant director: Karine van Greevenbroek. Design: Jago Bo. Assistant designer: Monika Bloch. Costumes: Elly Vermeulen. Stage manager: Pieter Rienks. Performances in the tent. 27 May–15 September 1985.

14. *Little Brothers (Broertjes)*
Performed by Frank, René, and Paul Prenen. Performances in the tent. 29 May–15 September 1985.

15. *The Coronation of Poppea*
(Same cast, etc., as no. 8, except Yolande and Cas alternated.) Lighting: Henk Veltkamp. Performances in a summer festival tent. 25 May–8 September 1985.

Also during the 1984–85 season:

Cas acted in *The Impresario of Smyrna* (an adaptation) by Carlo Goldoni, with the RO Theater Company, Rotterdam (Direction:

Karst Woudstra). Hans Man in't Veld developed a piece about unemployment, *On the Beach (Am Strand)*, with the company (and others) at the Deutsches Schauspielhaus, Hamburg.

1985–1986

1. *Romeo and Jeanette*
1 October–1 November 1985.

2. *Incidental Project—Junior Bar Association, 1985*
Performed by Hans, Shireen, Toon Agterberg, Judith Hees, Kenneth Herdigein, Lieneke le Roux, and Maarten Wansink. Research: Hans, and Kenneth Herdigein. 7 November 1985.

3. *Romeo and Jeanette*—Video film version
Performed by Shireen, Toon Agterberg, Judith Hees, Kenneth Herdigein, Lieneke le Roux, and Maarten Wansink. Direction: Jago Bo and Shireen. Lighting: Reinier van Brummelen, Thijs Struick, Sam Tjioe, and Peter van der Werf. Camera: Maarten Rens and Dorith Vinken. Sound: Marcel van Brummelen. Production coordinator: Maria Peters. Assistants: Monika Bloch, Rob Duyker, and Pieter Rienks. Catering: Lydia de Koning and Nicole van Vessum. Makeup: Leendert van Nimwegen. Montage: Sam Tjioe and Dorith Vinken. Videotaping: 11, 12, 13 November 1985.

4. *Laios*
Based on the Oedipus myth. Performed by Herman, Dick van Gendt, Sabine Heres, Neel Holst, Marc Krone, and Carla Reitsma. Direction: Yolande. Music: Hero Wouters. Design: Dieter Junker. Design assistant: Chris Richelman. Costumes: Yvonne de Boer and Jany Hubar (adviser). Technical work and lighting: Henk Veltkamp. Videotaping in rehearsal: Daria, and Henk Veltkamp. 11 January 1986–10 April 1987.

5. *Epiphany (Epifanie)*, based on the play *Epiphany*, by Lewis John Carlino
Performed by Frank and René. Direction: Michiel Berkel. Design, costumes: Hadassah Kann. Lighting: Reinier Tweebeeke. Technical work: Hans Looye. 20 January 1986–3 May 1986. (Continued independently from the Werkteater, 1986–87.)

6. *Absent Friends (Verre vrienden)*, by Alan Ayckbourn
Performed by Shireen, Toon Agterberg, Judith Hees, Ken-

neth Herdigein, Lieneke le Roux, and Maarten Wansink. Direction: Shireen. Design: Bram Vermeulen. Costumes: Elly Vermeulen. Technical work and lighting: Thijs Struick. Assistant: Pieter Rienks. 28 January 1986–15 June 1986.

7. *Incidental Project—Heart Foundation*, Video film
(Same cast as no. 2, 1984–85, except Kenneth Herdigein instead of Neel Holst.) Directors: Shireen, and Sam Tjioe. Costumes: Evelien Birza. Producer: Ted Dellen, Foundation for Film and Science. Videotaping 10, 11, 12, and 13 March 1986.

8. *"Tjapa," and Other Songs*, from "The Nursery," a song cycle by Moussorgsky—Video film
Performed by Caria van Slooten (boy), Alissa van Slooten (girl), and Robert Ouwerkerk (piano), Cari van Slooten (singing). Translation: Willem Wilmink. Video production: Daria, and Ruud Janssen. Sound: Leo van den Boogaard, Rein Hartog. Videotaping 1986.

9. *Incidental Project—Cross Foundation*
Performed by Shireen, Toon Agterberg, Judith Hees, Kenneth Herdigein, Lieneke le Roux, and Maarten Wansink. Music: Bram Vermeulen. Technical work and lighting: Thijs Struick. Research: Lieneke le Roux. 12 and 14 May 1986.

10. *Festin d'Esope*—Video film
Based on music by Charles-Valentin Alkan. Video production by Daria, Ruud Janssen, and Paul Prenen. Performed by Peter Blok, Rob Duyker, Flip Filz, Sabine Heres, Neel Holst, Jaap Hoogstra, Marc Krone, Paul Prenen, Carla Reitsma, and Hendrikje Wouters, with Paul Prenen (music), Greetje Bijma (singing), Henk Bakboord (dancing). Sound: Leo van den Boogaard. Lighting: Thijs Struick, Henk Veltkamp. Production Assistant: Judith van de Bos. Script: Martine Nijhoff. Catering: Evelien Birza. Videotaping 20–25 April 1986.

11. *The Rules of the House*—Video film
Based on the 1981–82 stage performance of *The Rules of the House*. Performed by Daria, Herman, Flip Filz, Arie Kant, and Carla Reitsma. Direction: Yolande. Scenario: Yolande, and Ineke van der Weele. Camera: Maarten Rens. Production Coordinator: Natasa Hanusova. Lighting: Thijs Struick, Henk Veltkamp. Sound: Leo van den Boogaard. Costumes: Evelien Birza. Decor/Set Dressing: Barbara de Vries. Catering: Karin Graven.

Music: Paul Prenen. Script: Martine Nijhoff. Assistants: Peter Blok, Sabine Heres, Marc Krone. Videotaping 7–22 June 1986.

Also in 1986:

There was a tour in Germany and Belgium of *You Are My Mother, Adio,* and *Absent Friends.*

NOTE: During the summer of 1986 there was no summer tent show.

B

Performances in International Festivals and Awards Received

Performances by the Werkteater in International Festivals

Festival Høvikodden, Oslo	1973
Festival Mondial du Théâtre, Nancy	1975
Norddeutsches Theatertreffen, Hamburg	1976
Belgrade International Theater Festival, Belgrade	1979
Theater der Nationen, Hamburg	1979
13e Rassegna Internationale dei Teatri Stabili, Florence	1980
London International Festival of Theatre, London	1981
Theater der Welt, Cologne	1981
Züricher Theater Spektakel, Zurich	1981
Internationales Kinder- und Jugend-Theatertreffen, West Berlin	1981
Theater der Nationen, Amsterdam	1982
Teatro Festival Parma, Parma	1983
Internationales Theater Festspiel, Munich	1985
Züricher Theater Spektakel, Zurich	1985
Theater '85, Hannover	1985

Awards to the Amsterdam Werkteater

1972–73 Albert van Dalsum Prize (for playmaking and for acting), for the theater project *In a Mess.*

1974–75 Defresne Prize (for playmaking or directing), for the theater project *Twilight* (cash prize donated by the Werkteater to the Dutch theater group GLTwee).

1975 Louis d'Or (Best Actor), to Peter Faber in *Twilight* (rejected by the Werkteater because the project was a combined effort).

1976 Best Film, Prix d'Italia della Rai, for the film *In a Mess.*

1979 First Prize, Bitef Festival, Yugoslavia, for the theater project *You've Got to Live with It.*

1979 Second Prize, General Category, Rehabilitation Film Festival, New York, for the film *In a Mess.*

1980 Bronze Leopard, International Film Festival, Locarno, for the film *In for Treatment.*

1980 Interdenominational Award, International Film Festival, Locarno, for the film *In for Treatment.*

1980 Best Program, Nipkow-Schijf (Nipkow TV Disk, Dutch television award), for the film *In for Treatment.*

1980 Best European TV Drama, Prix d'Italia della Rai, for the film *In for Treatment.*

1980 Outstanding Film of the Year, London Film Festival, for the film *In for Treatment.*

1981 Outstanding Film of the Year, Fifth Hong Kong International Film Festival, for the film *In for Treatment.*

1981 First Prize, International Red Cross and Health Film Festival, Varna, Bulgaria, for the film *In for Treatment.*

1982 Louis d'Or (Best Actor), to Joop Admiraal in *You Are My Mother.*

1983 Gold Medal, Adolf Grimme Preis (German), to Joop Admiraal for creating and performing *You Are My Mother.*

1984 Wilhelmina Luebke Preis (German), to Joop Admiraal for the film *Du bist meine Mutter* (*You Are My Mother*).

1983–84 Albert van Dalsum Prize, to Jan Ritsema for all of his work, including that as stimulator/director for *You Are My Mother* and *Adio* (prize rejected by Jan Ritsema, feeling he should not be singled out from among the collaborators on the projects).

1986 Adolf Grimme Preis (German), nomination to Cas Enklaar for the video production of *Visit with Joan.*

1986 Best TV Drama, Input Festival, Toronto, for the video production of *Visit with Joan.*

C

Dutch Text of
the Rense-Helmert Scene
in *Twilight*

RENSE

We gaan lekker in het zonnetje zitten hè. Zo. Hier is je plaatsje, hm. Kijk die zon nou es schijnen. Altijd in het voorjaar krijg ik datzelfde opwindende gevoel dat ik vroeger had als ik met mijn ouders naar dat kleine dorpje ging aan de voet van het duin. En dan stapten we in Amsterdam op de trein en dan zongen we de hele weg door.

(*Zingt.*)

Zoek de zon op, dat is zo fijn,
Want een beetje zonneschijn dat moet er zijn.

En dan in Alkmaar stapten we over op het stoomtrammetje.

HELMERT

Mijn vader hield helemaal niet van treinen. Hij zei dat ze niet bestonden. En dan wij als jongens hadden es een krant of tijdschrift waar een trein in stond en dat legden we hem voor en dan zeiden wij: Vader, dit is een trein! En dan werd hij vuurrood, stond op, pakte die krant van de tafel, liep naar de deur, draaide zich om en zei: Verraaiers! En dan ging hij naar het schijthuis en veegde zijn reet ermee af.

RENSE

En dan reed je. Onder een stralende hemel reed je langs het Noordhollands Kanaal. En dan bij de molen van Koedijk dan sloeg je af de polder in. En het was alsof een godenhand de weiden had volgestrooid met bloemen. En de vogeltjes waren in de lucht. En de sloten waren vol kroos en eenden.

For a discussion of this scene, see Chapter 4, "Playmaking: The Experience of the Actors."

HELMERT

De poldersloten waren wel vijf meter breed of meer. En dan waren er van die Brabanders—dat waren dagloners—en die hadden we in dienst en die trokken hun klompen uit, namen een aanloop en sprongen over die sloot heen! Vijf meter of meer! Mannetjesputters! God!

RENSE

En dan kwam je aan op dat kleine stationnetje onder de bomen. En dan stond Roland Holst daar met z'n stokje. En dan stapte je uit het trammetje en dan rook je de zeelucht, vermengd met die stoom van dat locomotiefje.

HELMERT

En dan was er een wijf onder die Brabanders, dat was een manwijf. Die kon vechten en werken gelijk de kerels. En als je d'r een kwartje gaf dan nam ze met d'r blote hand de ratten van de dorsvloer en beet ze de kop af! Aàh! Alsof ze een hap brood nam.

RENSE

En dan wandelden we door de duinen naar zee toe en het was eens op een dag en toen zagen we een konijntje hollen en wijken. Wij rennen, rennen, rennen er achteraan, en ik weet niet hoe het kwam, maar toen . . .

HELMERT

Zaterdag gingen de kinderen in bad. Dan werden ze allemaal bij elkaar gehaald. Dan werden de kleertjes uitgetrokken. Dan werden ze als jonge hondjes in de tobbe geplonsd, en dat spetterde en dat spatterde, dat maakte een plezier . . .

RENSE

Toen struikelde ik. Ik struikelde.

HELMERT

Laatst is er zo'n ventje van het dak gevallen.

RENSE

En er liep een klein straaltje over mijn kin en er kwamen grote rooie droppen op mijn witte pakje.

HELMERT

Ach jochie, kom maar. Kinderen moeten spelen. Die moeten niet ziek zijn. Kom maar hier, ventje, kom maar hier, m'n jochie. M'n kleintje.

En als ze ziek zijn dan houd je ze de hele dag bezig. Dan doe je het ene spelletje na het andere en je wordt eigenlijk niet vermoeid, want ze moeten er bovenop komen, die kleintjes. Dat ze weer kunnen spelen.

M'n jochie, ach jochie, m'n ventje. Je ruikt ziek zelfs. Je vader is er niet, je moeder is er niet, maar ik ben bij je. Dan word je weer fit, dan kun je weer spelen, hè. Spelen achter elkaar door.

(*Zingt.*)

Zo doet het herenpaard, en het herenpaard doet zó.
En zo doet het damespaard, en het damespaard doet
zó.
En zo doet het boerenpaard, en het boerenpaard doet
zó!

Index

The index does not incorporate material in the Appendixes and the play *Twilight*, nor does it include the actors' speech ascriptions in the Actors' Comments on *Twilight*. It does cover the rest of the book, including the texts of the Actors' Commentary, figure captions, and the notes.

Designer: Wolfgang Lederer
Compositor: G & S Typesetters, Inc.
Text: 11/13 Caledonia
Display: Caledonia
Printer: Braun-Brumfield, Inc.
Binder: Braun-Brumfield, Inc.

Performance Dynamics and the Amsterdam Werkteater

DUNBAR H. OGDEN

The Amsterdam Werkteater from 1970 to 1985 became the finest actors' theater in the Western world. Here the actor was first, on stage and off, as player, playwright, and director. Plays were created through a powerful, personal working relationship, like that of a great string quartet. While its methods were unusual, the Werkteater's principles were the most important principles of all theater in all ages.

This first major study, written for both the theatergoer and the creator of theater, documents the evolution of the play *Twilight*—presenting the text, an analysis of its development and significance, and detailed, often emotional comments from the actors about its creation and performance. Thus the troupe's experiences and ideas become accessible to theater students and aspiring actors.

Dunbar H. Ogden feels that the Werkteater has succeeded in returning the special power of theater to the actor. Through his intimate record of the troupe's work, he offers insight into what all great performers seek and many have achieved in all ages—that powerful current of electricity between actors and audience, drawn together by the basic human instinct for play.